Neither an autobiography nor a scholarly analysis, *Labor's Struggles, 1945–1950: A Participant's View* is a skillful blend of both genres. Informative and original in its insights and analyses, this book provides the reader with information available from no other source. These insights must be included in any subsequent efforts to interpret this period in labor history.

Richter based this account largely on his own experience as legislative representative for the United Auto Workers-CIO from 1943 to 1947, as well as on documents and conversations from that period, supplemented with historical research. Active in the effort to educate the working class on all important historical and legislative issues and on the political process, Richter wrote and lectured often for UAW and other union audiences and authored a syndicated column that was frequently featured on the front pages of local union papers and city and state central council papers.

This study of policy making in union headquarters and in Washington focuses on the 1945 splits within the CIO as well as the sharp divisions between the "social" CIO and the "opportunistic" AFL. In addition, it focuses on the Labor Management (Taft-Hartley) Act of 1947, which divided an already fragmented movement.

LABOR'S STRUGGLES, 1945–1950

LABOR'S STRUGGLES, 1945–1950

A Participant's View

IRVING RICHTER

CAMBRIDGE
UNIVERSITY PRESS

Published by the Press Syndicate of the University of Cambridge
The Pitt Building, Trumpington Street, Cambridge CB2 1RP
40 West 20th Street, New York, NY 10011-4211, USA
10 Stamford Road, Oakleigh, Melbourne 3166, Australia

© Cambridge University Press 1994

First published 1994

Printed in the United States of America

Library of Congress Cataloging-in-Publication Data
Richter, Irving.
Labor's struggles, 1945–1950 : a participant's view / Irving Richter.
p. cm.
ISBN 0-521-41412-1
1. Industrial relations – United States. 2. Labor – United States.
3. United States – Politics and government – 1945–1953. I. Title.
HD8072.5.R53 1994
331.88′0973 – dc20 91-33419
CIP

A catalog record for this book is available from the British Library.

ISBN 0521-41412-1 hardback

CONTENTS

FOREWORD

In June 1947 Congress passed the Taft-Hartley Act over the veto of President Harry S. Truman. The law consisted of a series of amendments to the Wagner Act of 1935. It retained the Wagner Act's framework of certification of unions through elections supervised by the National Labor Relations Board and its prohibitions against specified "unfair labor practices" through which employers attempted to prevent their workers from unionizing or tried to control unions, but it changed the thrust of the act by also outlawing such important union practices as closed shops, strikes in violation of contracts, mass picketing, secondary boycotts, and other actions of solidarity. It also banned union contributions to political candidates, forbad employees of the government from striking, permitted states to outlaw union security agreements, and authorized the president to seek a court injunction forbidding for eighty days any strikes that might affect national health or safety. Its most dramatic innovation was a requirement that no union could appeal to the protections of the law or the services of the NLRB unless its elected officers all signed affidavits stating that they were not members of the Communist Party.

Truman's veto message contended that the bill would "reverse the basic direction of our national labor policy, inject the government into private economic affairs on an unprecedented scale, and conflict with important principles of our democratic society."[1] Union rallies across the land denounced Taft-Hartley as a "slave-labor law" or, in the words of President John L. Lewis of the United Mine Workers, as "the first ugly, savage thrust of Fascism in America." The unprecedented size of the American union movement lent significance to those denunciations. In June 1947 fully 87 percent of all construction workers, 83 percent of all miners, 76 percent of railway workers, and 41 percent of workers in manufacturing belonged to unions, and during

[1]Samuel Eliot Morison and Henry Steele Commager, *Growth of the American Republic*, 5th ed. (New York, 1962), Vol. II, p. 855.

the preceding twelve months more NLRB certification elections (5,194) had
been won by unions than in any other year in the board's history. Seventy-
seven percent of the 805,000 eligible voters had cast their ballots in favor of
union representation.[2] Nevertheless, Congress handily overrode the presidential veto. Moreover, in 1949, despite Democratic majorities in both houses of
Congress, an attempt to repeal the law in fulfillment of the victorious party's
national platform was decisively defeated. Since that time Taft-Hartley has
remained, with but minor modifications (though after 1959 without the noncommunist affidavit), the uncontested law of the land.

Irving Richter was the legislative representative of the United Automobile
Workers of America (UAW) during the battle over this momentous legislation. His "participant's view" suggests that factional antagonisms in the labor
movement made possible the enactment, perpetuation, and enforcement of the
new law, and that the law itself (and especially the noncommunist affidavit)
aroused that factionalism to the point of debilitating the entire movement.
Moreover, he contends, the reshaping of the labor movement was inseparable
from the development of Cold War foreign policy.

Richter had acquired his position in the UAW as a result of many years of
government service and political activism. (Indeed, his recollections reveal
the importance of consultation between key government personnel and top
union leaders for all contending factions of the labor movement during the
1940s.) He had been graduated in 1934 from the University of Wisconsin,
where he had studied labor economics under the influential Selig Perlman,
and he had subsequently worked for New Deal relief agencies and the Labor
Department before becoming the auto workers' legislative representative and
director of political action. Like the union's general counsel, Maurice Sugar,
Richter was one of many union staff members who either joined the Communist Party or worked in close alliance with it. His columns on legislative
affairs were carried in many of the most important local union papers of the
UAW. Because he was an influential adviser to the administration of President
R. J. Thomas and Secretary-Treasurer George Addes, Richter was singled out
for attack as a communist by their rival Walter Reuther, who defeated Thomas
for the presidency in March 1946. As soon as Reuther's supporters gained
control of the UAW executive board in November 1947, he summarily dis-

---

[2]Melvyn Dubofsky and Warren Van Tine, *John L. Lewis: A Biography* (New York, 1977),
pp. 473–6; Leo Troy, "Rise and Fall of American Trade Unions: The Labor Movement from
FDR to RR," in Seymour Martin Lipset, ed., *Unions in Transition: Entering the Second Century*
(San Francisco, 1986), p. 87; Michael Goldfield, *Worker Insurgency, Radical Organization, and
New Deal Labor Legislation*, Occasional Paper No. 8, Center for Labor-Management Policy
Studies, City University of New York, p. 19.

missed both Richter and Sugar.[3] Richter subsequently managed election campaigns for Henry Wallace's Progressive Party and then operated his own
service company for trade unionists until 1963, when he went to England to
earn a Ph.D. in economics from Cambridge University. Thereafter he taught,
first at Mount Holyoke College and then at the University of the District of
Columbia, where he became an impressive and popular teacher, until his
retirement in 1984. After a protracted battle with cancer, he died in May
1989.

Richter finished writing *Labor's Struggles, 1945–1950: A Participant's
View* during the last months of his life. The book reflects his own unusual
experience and training as well as his determination to clarify the record of the
immediate postwar years, which critically shaped the character of the American labor movement and American social life. It is neither an autobiography
nor a scholarly analysis of the impact of the Cold War on the labor movement,
though it contains elements of both. Richter's book is more a study of policy
making in union headquarters and in Washington than social history or personal narrative. The author's presence in his story is evident more in his
selection of historical incidents for analysis than in discussion of his own
experiences. Richter has supplemented his own recollections, syndicated columns, diary excerpts, and extensive notes from the period with archival
research and a critical reading of influential studies written recently by such
historians as Nelson Lichtenstein, Bert Cochran, and Howell John Harris.[4]

Richter's View of the Reconversion Crisis

This unusual account of the disunity that made labor unions vulnerable to new
legal tethers just when they were enjoying their greatest popularity and effectiveness poses a serious challenge to historians who have interpreted the
postwar labor movement in terms of corporate liberalism, and also to those
who have depicted the policies of the Communist Party as the key to controversies inside the new industrial unions.[5] Some of the major arguments for-

[3]See Christopher H. Johnson, *Maurice Sugar: Law, Labor, and the Left in Detroit, 1912–1950*
(Detroit, 1988), pp. 286–98; Roger Keeran, *The Communist Party and the Auto Workers' Unions*
(New York, 1980), pp. 250–6, 261–5, 280–5; Bert Cochran, *Labor and Communism: The
Conflict That Shaped American Unions* (Princeton, N.J., 1977), pp. 257–63.
[4]Nelson Lichtenstein, *Labor's War at Home: The CIO and World War II* (Cambridge, 1982);
Cochran, *Labor and Communism;* Howell John Harris, *The Right to Manage: Industrial Rela-
tions Policies of American Business in the 1940s* (Madison, Wisc., 1982).
[5]On corporate liberalism, see Ronald Radosh, "The Corporate Ideology of American Labor,"
Studies on the Left, 6 (November–December 1966): 66–92, and a quite different conception in
Ronald W. Schatz, "Philip Murray and the Subordination of the Industrial Unions to the United

mulated by Richter run counter to widely accepted conceptions of the mid 1940s. Although many historians may not be fully persuaded by any or all of his arguments, anyone writing seriously about this epoch in the future will have to take them into account.

Richter's first contention is that the Labor-Management Charter, which spelled out conditions for postwar industrial peace, enjoyed little support in the unions and none worth mentioning in the business world. The charter presented to the public by President Eric Johnston of the U.S. Chamber of Commerce in the spring of 1945 had, Richter reveals, been drafted by two members of the United Steelworkers' office staff, Robert K. Lamb and Edith Pratt, who had worked with Johnston in the Committee for Economic Development.

To describe the charter as a futile endeavor is nothing new. Howell John Harris demonstrated persuasively that the charter had little influence on the business delegates to the president's Labor-Management Conference in November 1945. Those delegates, Harris argued, were truly representative of the business world and well briefed by the National Association of Manufacturers and the research of the Industrial Relations Counselors, to take the determined stand in favor of revision of the Wagner Act that Richter describes.[6] Moreover, Richter shows that the most serious practical effort to secure reconversion to a peacetime economy without strikes, Chester Bowles' plan for a 10 percent wage increase for all workers in return for a continuation of the unions' wartime no-strike pledge, did not meet with even President Truman's approval.[7]

More important than Richter's revelations about policy debates in Washington are his reasons (sometimes explicit and sometimes implicit) for shifting

States Government," in Melvyn Dubofsky and Warren Van Tine, eds., *Labor Leaders in America* (Urbana, Ill., 1987), pp. 234–57. For recent studies emphasizing the role of the Communist Party, see e.g. Lichtenstein, *Labor's War at Home;* Martin Glaberman, *Wartime Strikes: The Struggle Against the No-Strike Pledge in the UAW During World War II* (Detroit, 1980); Mike Davis, *Prisoners of the American Dream: Politics and Economy in the History of the U.S. Working Class* (London, 1986); Johnson, *Sugar;* Martin Halpern, *The Disintegration of the Left Coalition in the UAW, 1945–1950* (Albany, N.Y., 1987); Keeran, *The Communist Party and the Auto Workers' Unions* (Bloomington, Ind., 1980). On communists, see also Cochran, *Labor and Communism;* Harvey Klehr, *The Heyday of American Communism: The Depression Decade* (New York, 1984); Maurice Isserman, *Which Side Were You On? The American Communist Party During the Second World War* (Middletown, Conn., 1982).

[6]*The Right to Manage,* pp. 106–13. The Industrial Relations Counselors, Inc., had been created by John D. Rockefeller, Jr., in 1921 to advise business on labor strategies.

[7]For different versions of the failure of this effort, see Cochran, *Labor and Communism,* pp. 248–9, and Nelson Lichtenstein, "From Corporation to Collective Bargaining: Organized Labor and the Eclipse of Social Democracy in the Postwar Era," in Steve Fraser and Gary Gerstle, eds., *The Rise and Fall of the New Deal Order* (Princeton, N.J., 1989), pp. 122–52.

the focus of historical analysis away from the policies of the communists in the Congress of Industrial Organizations (CIO). The first is that unions outside of the CIO had no sympathy for schemes of strike-free, managed reconversion. The second is that the guiding force of CIO policy was not the communists, but President Philip Murray.

Although the charter had attested to management's "inherent right . . . to direct the operations of an enterprise," all labor representatives to the president's conference, including those of the CIO, rejected business' proposals for an explicit listing of management's rights. The officers of the American Federation of Labor (AFL), the railroad brotherhoods, and the United Mine Workers all opposed a national wage settlement or even discussion of the wage question. They all insisted on unrestricted collective bargaining. John L. Lewis of the miners denounced efforts to link negotiated wage increases to the cost of living, saying, "We say we are for free enterprise. We are opposed to the corporate state and all its manifestations as expressed in the CIO resolution."[8]

Richter thus reminds us that the CIO in 1945 was a minority force in the union movement despite its decisive importance in such major industries as steel, autos, and electrical machinery, representing fewer than 6,000,000 out of 14,800,000 organized workers. The AFL unions have attracted far too little attention from historians of the war and postwar years, even though four of the five citywide general strikes of 1946 were initiated by AFL affiliates.[9] The support those strikes enjoyed from CIO members in the cities where they took place, and the role of AFL members like the New York longshoremen and the San Francisco machinists in initiating the postwar strike wave (in both those cases through wildcat actions) underscore the weakness of any interpretation of the labor movement based solely on the words and deeds of leaders of either the CIO or the AFL.

Moreover, the policy of the CIO itself was shaped by the United Steelworkers and its president, Philip Murray, to a degree that is seldom perceived by authors who focus on the battles between communists and their foes in the auto and electrical workers' unions. Murray and his union had not only

---

[8]*New York Times*, November 9, 1945, as quoted by Richter.
[9]Stamford, Rochester, Lancaster, and Oakland. The Pittsburgh strike was started by an independent union. See George Lipsitz, *Class and Culture in Postwar America: "A Rainbow at Midnight"* (South Hadley, Mass., 1982), pp. 37–86; Howard Kimeldorf, *Reds or Rackets? The Making of Radical and Conservative Unions on the Waterfront* (Berkeley and Los Angeles, 1988), pp. 154–5. A splendid study of the AFL has been written by Christopher L. Tomlins: "AFL Unions in the 1930s: Their Performance in Historical Perspective," *Journal of American History*, 65 (March 1979): 1021–42.

spawned the ill-fated Labor-Management Charter but also been the driving force behind the much more successful Political Action Committee (PAC). The PAC was formed by the CIO, under the leadership of Sidney Hillman, in order to help reelect President Franklin D. Roosevelt in 1944 as well as to defeat special enemies of labor and elect friends in congressional and state campaigns. Many historians have agreed with Bert Cochran that "the PAC was a powerhouse" of decisive importance in several industrial states, soon imitated by the American Federation of Labor, and "laid the foundation for the modern labor bloc in American politics."[10] Quite different is the impression left by Richter, who describes nominal participation by the UAW's top officers and scarcely concealed disregard of the PAC by the ambitious Reuther, who was determined to develop his own independent ties to the Michigan Democratic Party.

Two historians have provided a useful context in which to situate Richter's recollection of the PAC. Mark McColloch has demonstrated that the United Steelworkers poured money and salaried staff into the PAC in 1944, with dramatic success in wards where steel workers resided, and that that union incessantly linked the achievement of its social goals to the war leadership of President Roosevelt. In 1943 it had demanded a "substantial down payment on the Four Freedoms," starting with democracy in the American South and national planning for postwar prosperity.[11] But Nelson Lichtenstein observes that "the grand effort to link a progressive social program to the wartime mobilization effort had proved unsuccessful by 1943, and Reuther had the political intelligence to recognize this failure earlier than most CIO leaders."[12] These differing perceptions help us not only understand why Reuther was not chosen by Murray to be one of the CIO delegates to the 1945 Labor-Management Conference but also, and more important, the role of the inadequately studied Steelworkers as the balance wheel of CIO policy.

The Great Strike Wave and Taft-Hartley

In the year following Japan's surrender, more than 4,600,000 American workers went on strike. Although most of the action was concentrated between

---

[10]Cochran, *Labor and Communism,* pp. 242, 243. Cochran's evaluation does slight the precedents of AFL political action in the 1906 and 1908 elections and the Conference for Progressive Political Action in 1922.

[11]"Consolidating Industrial Citizenship: The USWA at War and Peace, 1939–46," in Paul F. Clark, Peter Gottlieb, and Donald Kennedy, eds., *Forging a Union of Steel* (Ithaca, N.Y., 1987), pp. 83–4; "What Are We Fighting For?" *Steel Labor,* May 28, 1943, pp. 6–7.

[12]Lichtenstein, *Labor's War at Home,* p. 149.

January and April of 1946, when the CIO's steel workers, auto workers, electrical workers, and packinghouse workers all conducted industrywide strikes, the work stoppages had begun in maritime and shipbuilding occupations and later brought out all the coal miners and, briefly in May, every railroad worker in the land. Richter depicts labor's posture during these strikes as "largely defensive." He agrees with Murray's judgment that business wanted to maximize industrial turmoil in order to generate congressional support for new legislation to rein in unions. He illustrates the point by recalling the Republicans' 1946 campaign slogan denouncing "Communism, Confusion, and Chaos" and by recounting at length the use made of the controversial strike of United Auto Workers Local 248 at Allis-Chalmers by the House committee preparing the Taft-Hartley bill.

Richter's view of the 1946 strike is unlikely to be considered adequate by many historians. It is at this point that a view from Washington imposes the most restrictive blinkers. Other historians have noted that the strikes of rubber workers, machinists, dockers, and others in September and October 1945 were galvanized by enthusiasm for a 30 percent wage increase (forty-eight hours' pay for forty hours' work), which union officers could not restrain. Competing unions and leadership factions scrambled to identify themselves with the workers' hunger for a major and immediate improvement in their standard of living. This competition doomed not only Murray's dream of a government-imposed national settlement but also the efforts of the United Electrical Workers (UE) to coordinate the struggles of all CIO unions around concerted actions and demands. Previously unorganized workers by the hundreds of thousands became union members during the strikes. Ultimately Murray's Steelworkers called out 400,000 workers in the largest single strike in American history. And, unlike the industry's strikes of 1919 and 1937, it was not challenged by a single strikebreaker. In the months following the strike Murray dismissed his own union's aides who had been the most ardent enthusiasts of labor-management cooperation, Clinton Golden, Joseph Scanlon, and Harold Ruthenberg, and castigated their celebrated proposals.[13]

Nevertheless, many historians would agree with Richter that business also took the offensive in 1946. They would locate that attack, however, in the

[13]Cochran, *Labor and Communism,* pp. 248–50; Lipsitz, *Class and Culture,* pp. 37–55; Art Preis, *Labor's Giant Step: Twenty Years of the CIO* (New York, 1972), pp. 257–86; James J. Matles and James Higgins, *Them and Us: Struggles of a Rank-and-File Union* (Englewood Cliffs, N.J., 1974), pp. 137–49; McColloch, "Consolidating Industrial Citizenship," p. 54; Lichtenstein, *Labor's War at Home,* pp. 216–30; Jeremy Brecher, *Strike!* (San Francisco, 1972), pp. 226–30; comments of John Hoerr and Harold J. Ruttenberg, in Clark, Gottlieb and Kennedy, eds., pp. 120–9.

workplace, as well as in the committee rooms of Congress. Rulings by government agencies had significantly increased the authority of union representatives and regulations on the job, initiated the process of reducing (though not abolishing) wage differentials based on region, race, and gender, strengthened the institutional security of unions, and encouraged industrywide collective bargaining, while the high wartime demand for labor had enabled unions to ease piecework standards and had encouraged militancy in the workplace. Employers' efforts to roll back these gains generated some of the most intense conflicts of that year – and of subsequent years.[14] Although none of these observations refute Richter's participant's view, they do suggest a need to supplement it with other perspectives.

Finally, Richter has argued that labor's resistance to the Taft-Hartley law was far less forceful than the speeches and resolutions at union conventions suggest. The noncommunist affidavit provided a weapon for use against foes within the union movement that was too tempting for most officials to resist. Despite the widespread refusal of left-Wingers to submit their political views to government approval, and in defiance of the eloquent appeals of John L. Lewis and President J. Woodruff Randolph of the century-old Typographical Union that the unions repudiate all government interference in the workers' movement by simply refusing to sign and operating, as they had before 1935, without certification, most union officers hastened to sign. CIO unions whose officers initially refused to sign, like the electrical, farm equipment, packinghouse, and wood workers, found themselves raided by AFL (and eventually other CIO) unions whose names could appear on NLRB ballots, whereas those of nonconformists could not. Supporters of Walter Reuther confronted their rivals personally in local meetings and at the 1947 UAW convention, demanding that they sign. In 1949 when the CIO expelled eleven member unions as "communist-dominated," their early refusal to comply with Taft-Hartley was taken in evidence.

Moreover, few unions chose to hazard life without NLRB protection (and in defiance of NLRB rulings), no matter how obnoxious they found the new legal restraints that came with that protection. This was made clear by the AFL's response to Taft-Hartley. Lewis' summons to the 1947 convention to

---

[14]Harris, *The Right to Manage*, pp. 56–8, 152; David Brody, *Workers in Industrial America: Essays on the Twentieth Century Struggle* (New York, 1980), pp. 173–91; Ruth Milkman, *Gender at Work: The Dynamics of Job Segregation by Sex During World War II* (Urbana, Ill., 1987); Ronald W. Schatz, *The Electrical Workers: A History of Labor at General Electric and Westinghouse, 1923–60* (Urbana, Ill., 1983).

ignore the affidavits and the board was answered by the Federation's secretary-treasurer, George Meany. In a speech that made him heir apparent to Federation president William Green, Meany first recounted the practical problems any modern union would face if it defied the government, and then proclaimed himself ready to sign not only the required affidavit but also another stating "that I was never a comrade to the comrades."[15]

Rejecting defiance, labor could hope only for repeal of the new law. That aspiration tied unions more closely yet to the Democratic Party and to its foreign policy. At Meany's urging, the AFL formed Labor's League for Political Education to strengthen its political alliances and influence, while the CIO expelled any affiliated union that failed to support Truman's reelection campaign. Despite their campaign promises, the Democrats in Congress brought to the floor a bill that actually retained several restrictive features of the new law, and then failed to muster the votes to pass even that. After the outbreak of the Korean War, repeal efforts only singled out specific features of the law. Union practice accommodated itself to the strictures of the law (except in the building trades), just as dominant union ideologies adhered to Cold War anticommunism.

Christopher L. Tomlins has concluded, in a recent history of labor and the law, that the "Taft-Hartley Act . . . proved much less of a break with the past than has usually been assumed."[16] He presents in evidence the increasingly restrictive pattern of development in NLRB rulings before 1947 and the basic consistency between board rulings before and since the enactment of Taft-Hartley. Richter's participant's view has a larger focus: It is concerned with the law's role in restraining the power of organized workers at the moment it had reached full flood and in encouraging within the union movement debilitating factionalism and repression.

Despite their disagreements in interpreting the past, both Tomlins and Richter are aware of the importance of this historical controversy for contemporary politics. In recent years a sense of crisis has informed the labor movement's debates over its own future and has encouraged the questioning of beliefs and practices that have been immune to challenge since the epoch of the noncommunist affidavit. Irving Richter's parting thoughts and recollections can contribute not only to historical revision but also to the renewal of the union

---

[15]Robert H. Zieger, "George Meany: Labor's Organization Man," in Dubofsky and Van Tine, eds., *Labor Leaders*, p. 334.
[16]*The State and the Union: Labor Relations, Law, and the Organized Labor Movement in America, 1880–1960* (Cambridge, 1985), p. 251.

movement, just as his earlier legislative work helped fashion its vigorous past.[17]

DAVID MONTGOMERY

Yale University

---

[17]I am deeply indebted to Amy Stanley for providing me with information about Richter's career and to Nelson Lichtenstein for his critical comments on a draft of this foreword.

PREFACE AND ACKNOWLEDGMENTS

This book has had a long gestation period. It probably began in 1931, when I first became a dissident at the University of Wisconsin. In 1933, when Hitler came to power in Germany, I was in the classes of both John R. Commons and Selig Perlman. The former was ending a distinguished career as an economic theorist, reformer, and labor historian. Perlman, Commons' disciple and already an eminent labor academician, was carrying on the "Wisconsin School" tradition: featuring the local union of the American Federation of Labor as the preferred model of labor organizations, frowning on industrial forms of organizations as dangerous, discouraging labor union involvement in politics.

At Wisconsin in the 1880s, Commons' mentor Richard T. Ely had been placed on trial before the Board of Regents for discussing the subjects of socialism and trade unionism. In the early 1930s, it was no longer daring or risky for an academic to discuss AFL-style unionism or to give a course on capitalism, socialism, and communism, as Professor Perlman did each year. But Perlman made clear his strong disapproval of ideas popular in the 1930s with many undergraduates: mass or open unionism, radical politics, and a labor party.

I had then, and have now, great respect for Perlman's insights. I am sure they influenced my own later views. Indeed, several influential critics of my *Political Purpose in Trade Unions* (published in 1973 from my doctoral dissertation at Cambridge University) viewed that book as a Perlmanish interpretation of American and British trade union attitudes toward politics.

While Perlman did indeed influence me and, much more so, the men and women who were my classmates as well as succeeding generations of scholars and trade union leaders and staffers, I have come to see his published views as provocative and thoughtful but highly subjective. I believe Selig Perlman's theory of the labor movement was shaped by his bitter experiences as a socialist under the Polish colonels, and then by his fears of what might happen to him as a Jew and former radical if U.S. labor should take the advice of radicals ("intellectuals") and launch into industrial-type unions.

As a young man in pre–World War I Poland, Perlman had joined the socialists, probably through the Jewish Bund. After coming to the United States and securing acceptance at an institution of higher learning that was progressive enough to be studying labor and unionism, he decided to combat the notion – widespread in the 1920s and early 1930s – that the American Federation of Labor, which the Wisconsin School had come to admire, should be broadened by dropping its craft philosophy and embracing industrial unionism. This scared him. Prophetically, he saw that such forms of mass unionism, by opening the door to minorities and to unskilled and semiskilled workers, would bring a backlash. To survive, such a movement would be forced into political action. The combination of labor politics and mass unionism would be too much for "the bosses." Professor Perlman believed that most American employers, frightened by such a power shift, would simply not accept broader organizational activity, even where they had come to live with the more limited craft-style unions. "It will only arouse the sleeping dogs of fascism," I recall his telling a class at Madison in his heavily accented English.

A similar proposition, in modified form, was incorporated in Perlman's classic *Theory of the Labor Movement*. This *Theory* is considered again in Chapter 1 of the present study. It is to be noted here that while the CIO succeeded in organizing and gaining contracts in mass-production industries, the leading employer organization, the National Association of Manufacturers, was and remains opposed, in principle, to all forms of unionism.

In 1934, B.A. in hand, I hopped a freight car to Washington, then the promised land of the New Deal, and won an appointment in the Federal Emergency Relief Administration (FERA).

From FERA I went to the Works Progress Administration (WPA) and then to the Labor Department as an economist. In addition to these paid jobs, I worked at FERA, WPA, and Labor as a local union organizer and officer for the American Federation of Government Employees, AFL.

My full-time CIO connection began in 1943 when I became the national legislative representative of the United Auto Workers, a job I viewed as part of the great CIO crusade on behalf of the heretofore neglected mass-production workers. I joined, loudly, in the hosannas for the "labor movement." However, I realized very soon after starting work on Capitol Hill for the UAW-CIO – although I never said so publicly – that the new CIO movement had nothing in common, socially or politically, with the American

Federation of Labor. I was very proud of carrying the CIO banner for what I regarded as its objective of not only organizing but representing in politics the open, mass unions; in my mind, the CIO and its affiliates stood for full and equal opportunity for political, racial, and religious minorities; for social reform; and for the defeat of Nazism and fascism. But because I was identifying with the left-center caucus in the UAW that I then considered to be on the side of the angels, I was fired in late 1947 when a right-wing group won power in the UAW and the CIO as a whole decided it was no longer opportune to be seen standing alongside lefties and radicals, including people known as communists, under the old united-front banner.

The pages that follow represent my own perspective on events of 1945–50, a turning point in postwar labor history. My perspective is based on prior study of, and activity in, AFL and CIO unions; extended shop work; and graduate study at American and Columbia Universities as well as five years of close observation and participation in events in Washington for the UAW (1943–7). Fortunately, I kept some records of my own and do not have to rely on my own and other people's fading memories.

All this study and experience – and thought – have given me a particular place in the "historical procession," and "an angle of vision," to borrow two phrases from Cambridge professor E. H. Carr:

> The historian is just another dim figure trudging along in another part of the procession. And as the procession winds along, swerving now to the right and now to the left, sometimes doubling back on itself; the relative position of the different parts of the procession is constantly changing . . . new vistas, new angles of vision, constantly appear as the process – and the historian with it – moves along. The historian is part of the history. The point in the procession at which he finds himself determines his angle of vision over the past.[1]

In these pages, my angle of vision necessarily intrudes on both my selection of facts and my interpretation of those facts.

Notwithstanding Selig Perlman's admonitions, as soon as I became legislative representative of the auto union in the spring of 1943, I was ready to use political action for advancing what I considered the interests of the "working class" and the "labor movement." I was dedicated to the job, which in my view meant educating the rank and file on all important historical and legislative issues and on the political process. I wrote and lectured often for UAW and other union audiences about legislative procedures in Washington as well as the nuts and bolts of political action. My syndicated column was frequently

---

[1] Edward Hallett Carr, *What Is History?* (New York: Random House, 1961), pp. 42–3.

featured on the front page in local union and city and state central council
papers, and occasionally in the Negro and foreign-language press. I was also
persuasive with members of Congress and government officials in describing
the war role of labor. I was good at my work. My column was mainly placed
in so-called left-wing papers, but many of my most avid readers and vocal
supporters were so-called right-wingers. Most were no-wingers.

The political orientation of all my work in Washington and elsewhere was
consistent with CIO policy. At that time, I, along with most leftists and
centrists, worked closely with the large and vigorous communist group. I
knew and respected most of the Communist Party functionaries. When the
Communist Party moved to a position opposed by the UAW or CIO, however,
I ceased to be even a fellow traveler.

Communism loomed large in unions during the focal period of this study.
Yet communism, as theory or practice, was not advanced or even debated by
Communist Party members or others at UAW local meetings or at any other
union level, at least to my knowledge. The longer-established American Federation of Labor still considered CIO PAC-style political action as "red."
Political action was still suspect among workers generally. Even in the UAW,
the largest and politically one of the most active CIO affiliates, where some
officers tried to overcome suspicions about American politics, factional motivation (internal politics) was a constant: in the UAW's attitude toward political action and political parties, in the hiring and firing of staff representatives
and technicians, and even in its approaches to strikes and labor law, as I show
in later chapters.

During the 1943–4 presidential campaign, the auto workers' union seemed
to act as one unit for the reelection of Roosevelt; indeed, it was often cited by
CIO Political Action Committee (CIO PAC) officials as a model for political
actions.

This was an illusion, however. While the top officers, George F. Addes and
R. J. Thomas, accepted positions and performed significant, and unpaid,
duties with the national office of the CIO PAC, and were ostensibly part of a
broad united front with the left wing of the CIO, they showed little enthusiasm
or understanding for the undertaking. By contrast, Vice-President Walter
Reuther, who did indeed have a full understanding of the political implications
of the CIO, was in fact aloof from the CIO PAC because of the contemporaneous factional alignments in his own UAW and the CIO.

Addes and Thomas, who carried the ball for the UAW at the national
Political Action Committee, had some nonpolitical motivations. First, the
political channel could be urged as a plausible alternative to restless local

unionists chafing under the restrictions imposed by the wartime no-strike pledge, which was unanimously approved by all UAW officers but was by 1943 a special burden for all officers in the left-center coalition; second, PAC work now carried with it far more prestige than the organizing and negotiating tasks associated with the early days of the UAW and CIO (I recall arranging a luncheon at the Capitol for R. J. Thomas, who as PAC spokesman basked in and clearly relished the company of Clare Luce and about forty other members of Congress); third, and possibly most important, Addes and Thomas knew that the CIO PAC was the special interest of Sidney Hillman and that the PAC was also supported by Philip Murray. The latter two, as vice-presidents of the CIO under John L. Lewis, had been at the very center of auto worker financing and growth, and they were still expected to be speakers at UAW conventions, where their influence could be decisive in the many close and divisive questions and candidacies facing UAW delegates.

In practice, the Reuther-led coalition, comprising about half the UAW membership and staff, stood apart from both Hillman and the CIO PAC. Indeed, as is shown later, this opposition half of the union until 1948 frequently actively opposed the CIO PAC and its leaders, even though Walter Reuther himself fully understood labor's need for political allies in Washington and elsewhere.

The changes in the thinking of labor leaders and in the labor movement generally reflected those in the broader society. The roughly fifteen million adults who were members of labor organizations in 1945 rarely saw themselves as part of a movement. The AFL, unaffiliated labor unions, and the CIO were in fact sharply divided. One central point of this book is that even the CIO, the most "social" of the labor bodies and on the whole quite deeply involved in political action, was itself split on the Taft-Hartley labor law and other vital questions confronting organized labor in the period, far more so than might appear from the records.

The 1945 splits within the CIO, the division between the "social" CIO and the "opportunistic" AFL, the militant "free enterprise" leadership given to the miners by Lewis – all working without coordination or cooperation – prevented a postwar labor position from going forward to Congress, to the president, to the secretary of labor, or to the various union memberships. Similar splits occurred not only during the "slave-labor" bill but also over the great strike wave of 1945–6, which in turn helped usher in the Congress that enacted Taft-Hartley. The final two chapters of this book will focus on the Labor Management Relations (Taft-Hartley) Act of 1947, which seemed to unite, but actually further divided, an already fragmented movement.

Acknowledgments

Although I question some labor sources, many useful public and private records do exist. I have my own records and some memory of events. I have cited many archival and library sources that contain the papers of, and oral interviews with, major actors of the period. I spent many hours with union people and conducted many interviews. I have also consulted many books and articles by authors who have studied one phase or another of the period. I trust that my notes give sufficient credit to all the people who helped me. Some who helped prefer to remain unmentioned. I thank them all. I owe a special debt, also, to the following individuals for having read, edited, and commented on my manuscript or parts of it: Peter Agree, Pat Aufderheide, James Billington, George W. Crockett, Jr., Hasea and Steven Diner, Kathleen Dockett, Elizabeth and Mark Eudey, Steve Fraser, Irene Gordon, Herbert Hill, Noelle McAfee, Richard Sasuly, the late Rexford Tugwell and the staff of the Center for the Study of Democratic Institutions at Santa Barbara, and the late F. Palmer Weber. I owe a special debt to my lifelong friend Harold G. Vatter for his comments, encouragement, assistance, and questioning. My wife, Jeanne, has been a source of critical comments, love, patience, and total support.

I received, and gratefully acknowledge, financial help from the Ford Foundation, the University of the District of Columbia, and the Woodrow Wilson Center for International Studies.

I am grateful to the Library of Congress for granting me extended scholarly privileges and space.

1

LABOR'S FRAGMENTATION AND THE INDUSTRIAL RELATIONS CONTEXT IN 1945

Labor's Power

At the end of World War II, labor's aggregate numbers suggested real power. Many experts believed that the balance of power had shifted away from the management side to labor. In an address to a Princeton University conference in 1946, an eminent labor economist, Professor Sumner H. Slichter, placed trade union organizations in the context of what he called "a revolutionary shift in power from business to labor in the United States. . . . A laboristic society is succeeding a capitalistic one."[1]

Slichter's judgment was mirrored not only in economic, industrial, and historical studies but also, more significantly, in committees of Congress. When the 80th Congress decided in 1947 to reverse the basic New Deal labor law, the National Labor Relations (Wagner) Act, it did so partly on the ground that the "excessive power" of labor demanded statutory change. The law that the 80th Congress enacted in place of the Wagner Act, the Labor Management Relations (Taft-Hartley) Act, is still the basic labor law of the United States.

The concept of "Big Labor," originating in the 1940s, became an important argument for labor-law reversal. It has since become a fashionable term, connoting equal power, along with "Big Business" and "Big Government," with liberals as well as conservatives practicing this new addition to the American language.[2]

---

[1]Sumner H. Slichter, *Trade Unions in a Free Society* (Cambridge, Mass.: Harvard University Press, 1947), p. 5.

[2]E.g., *Bill Moyers' Journal*, WNET-TV, February 22, 1976, "Reflections on a Revolution," printed transcript, pp. 6–7, 10.

For an excellent summary of various recent modern theories of power, mainly those written from a Marxist and neo-Marxist perspective, see Douglas W. Dowd, *The Twisted Dream: Capitalist Development in the United States since 1776* (Cambridge, Mass.: Winthrop, 1977), pp. 271ff.

For other significant academic studies, see Adolph A. Berle, *Power* (New York: Harcourt Brace, 1967); Dudley W. Buffa, *Union Power and American Democracy* (Ann Arbor: University

1

The present book covers some relevant events of 1948–50, focusing however on the period 1945–7, a turning point in modern labor history. The latter three years include the final year of the Second World War, the early reconversion from a wartime to a peacetime economy, including the greatest strike wave in the history of the United States, and a change in the basic labor law of the United States.

Even under the present revised labor law, the federal system of the United States government leaves to the states wide jurisdiction over matters relating to labor. Nevertheless, the key to understanding postwar labor power rests on national developments in labor unionism itself, in national economic relations between management and labor, and in congressional actions in the field of labor legislation. This study, accordingly, emphasizes union political behavior as seen from a national perspective.

The central thesis of the study may be stated in two related propositions. First, contrary to the widespread impression that the unions were powerful in economic and political terms during the postwar period and in subsequent years, this book shows that American unions actually were fragmented and divided both as to political policy and basic wage policy. Second, organized employers were highly motivated and showed extraordinary organizing and political skills and solidarity, enabling industry to achieve in 1947 a basic reversal of the New Deal trend toward federal encouragement of labor unions and collective bargaining among equals. A brief description of the historical setting for the period will illuminate the meaning of the thesis, indicating how relationships developed among the actors in the industrial relations system: the unions, government, and employers.

During the rapidly developing but still early industrialization era (ca. 1886–1930), the central American Federation of Labor (AFL) and its affiliated labor unions enjoyed very little acceptance. They had been able to organize only a small proportion of eligible labor. And unlike the Trades Union Congress (TUC) of Great Britain, which had been a model for the strategic leaders of the AFL when they created an American counterpart in 1881–6, these early American unions – largely made up of skilled artisans – generally avoided political action. As Selig Perlman, the eminent theorist of the labor movement expressed it, the American labor unions functioned in a "fragile" environment

of Michigan Press, 1983); Neil W. Chamberlain, "Organized Labor: A Diminishing Force?" *Challenge,* January 1960, pp. 12–15. George Meany, who as president of the AFL-CIO and in prior positions in the AFL had placed himself squarely in the establishment, told an AFL-CIO executive council meeting in February 1979 that he feared "the end of representative government" if the political power of giant corporations should continue unchecked.

and rightly feared that if they entered into national partisan politics the unions would upset a delicate equilibrium.[3]

By common understanding of the locally based, craft-oriented unions that formed the original American Federation of Labor, the new labor federated body would grant national charters based on "exclusive jurisdiction" over designated crafts. The individual labor affiliates would bargain with their respective employers and also make their own rules on controlling entry into the trades and into membership. Thus, the Federation evolved into an essentially exclusionist as well as monopolistic labor group, its philosophy based on restricting the number of skilled people allowed to represent each trade. This could offer artisans the advantages that would come from controlling jobs against less skilled workers seeking to "dilute" the labor supply. Although the AFL-affiliated unions thereby narrowly limited their memberships and rejected reformism and socialism, the Federation became the main central body of unions engaged in collective, as against individual, bargaining.

In a predominantly laissez-faire economy, even limited collective bargaining aroused opposition not only from employers but also from agencies of government, including the courts. Governmental attitudes were to change with the advent of Franklin Roosevelt's New Deal. But the opposition of industrialists to collective bargaining, as represented by their leading organization, the National Association of Manufacturers, was only modified by economic and political conditions and never changed into full acceptance of the collective bargaining principle.[4]

In Britain, from the late nineteenth century to the immediate post–Second World War years, employer associations in the industrialized sectors were weaker in general than in the USA. British employers early recognized and adapted to union organization among hourly workers. By contrast, American employers were strong and unified, and they rallied behind their associations first to prevent and then to beat back organizing efforts. Long before American industrial workers developed an enduring industrial form – as against a

---

[3]Selig Perlman, *A Theory of the Labor Movement* (New York: Macmillan, 1928), ch. 5. Cf. Irving Richter, *Political Purpose in Trade Unions* (London: Allen & Unwin, 1973); Marc Karson, *American Labor Unions and Politics, 1900–1918* (Boston: Beacon, 1945).

[4]For organized industry's perspective as of 1962, see National Association of Manufacturers, *Economic Implications of Union Power*. This pamphlet contains a fundamental challenge to the principles of collective bargaining. In that sense it is a reversion to the founding views of the NAM and is at odds with the position the NAM took in 1945 at the president's Labor-Management Conference, where it appeared to accept the principle of collective bargaining and wished merely to reverse some of the gains made by labor. This 1945 role of the NAM, discussed briefly below and more fully in Chapter 2, was clearly a temporary expedient.

craft form – of unionization for collective bargaining, the employers formed their own organizations to coordinate their strategies against all forms of collective action by their employees.

The National Association of Manufacturers and Employer Solidarity

The original purpose of the National Association of Manufacturers (NAM) when it was organized in 1895 was to expand trade possibilities for its business members. The goal was changed, however, in less than a decade. According to Senators Robert M. La Follette and Elbert Thomas, the NAM shifted its basic purpose in 1903; from then on, its central aim became, in the words of La Follette's Committee on Education and Labor, "a belligerent opposition to union organization."[5]

During the First World War, government and industry allowed and even favored bargaining rights for, and accorded legitimacy to, the affiliated unions of the American Federation of Labor and to the AFL itself. Sam Gompers suddenly became a "labor statesman." As soon as the war was ended, however, the NAM reverted to the basic objective the industrial corporations had assigned to it in the prewar years of industrialization: to bar collective bargaining and restore individual bargaining without the intervention of labor organizations. The NAM's famous American Plan, a euphemism for the open shop – which in itself was a code word to bar employment to all potential unionists – was so successful that in the 1920s the general public came to regard unionism as unpatriotic.

The presidential election of 1932 gave new impetus to the NAM act on behalf of employers organized to resist trade unionism. Again according to La Follette, the Association, "because of its organization and experience," was chosen by leading manufacturers in Detroit and New York to lead a campaign called "national salvation." And the president of the Association defined for his members the legislative tasks visualized for the Association: "We are of course primarily committed to seeking the repeal of Section 7(a) of the National Industrial Recovery Act (NIRA)."[6] This provision, added under pressure from the AFL-affiliated and independent unions then in existence, re-

[5]U.S. Congress, Senate, Committee on Education and Labor, *Violations of Free Speech and Rights of Labor* (pursuant to S. Res. 266, 74th Cong.), 76th Cong., 1st sess., August 14, 1939, Report no. 6, pt. 6, *Labor Policies of Employers' Associations,* Part III: *The National Association of Manufacturers,* pp. 7, 81.
[6]Ibid., pp. 81, 208–12.

quired employers covered by NIRA codes to deal with their workers through unions of their own choosing.

Thus, as the federal government began its historic moves toward a mixed economy, organized industry was rallying to prevent a change in labor policies, specifically to avoid collective bargaining. To lead that campaign, the brass hats of corporate America chose the NAM, which became "The Voice of American Industry." Through the 1930s and 1940s, in the words of the La Follette Committee, the NAM's purpose was "to crush labor organizations formed by workers in their plants."[7] The NAM intensified its efforts after the NIRA was declared unconstitutional and Congress enacted, in place of Section 7(a), the National Labor Relations (Wagner) Act of 1935.

Of course, the NAM and NAM-created organizations, such as the Chamber of Commerce of the United States and the National Industrial Conference Board, were not the only business organizations interested in discouraging labor organizations. The National Metal Trades Association and the National Founders Association had been active in this regard for years before 1932. The point to note here is that as far back as the 1930s the NAM had been the leading coordinating employer association directing campaigns to reduce or eliminate altogether the collective power of workers in industry.[8]

Partly because its affiliated unions came mainly from the handicraft sectors and not from the manufacturing sectors, and functioned by "exclusive jurisdiction" granted them over crafts rather than plants, the AFL found it difficult to accommodate its structure and methods to match the growing employer offensives. Yet, even as the Federation continued to be dominated by craftsmen, it was also being called upon to organize mass-production workers (largely unskilled and foreign-born) in the fast-growing basic industries.

CIO-Style Unionism

The Federation's inability or refusal to adapt its structure to changing worker needs led in 1935 to a new central labor organization, the Congress of Industrial Organizations (CIO), chaired by John L. Lewis, the most charismatic and

---

[7]Ibid. Cf. National Association of Manufacturers, *Proceedings of the 12th Annual Convention* (1916), Committee on Resolutions reporting on "Industrial Peace," summarized and quoted in Robert A. Brady, *Business as a System of Power* (New York: Columbia University Press, 1943), p. 278.

[8]It is pertinent to emphasize – in view of CIO efforts in 1945 to enlist the aid of the Chamber of Commerce against what the CIO regarded as the aggressiveness of the NAM in seeking to change the Wagner Act – that the Chamber was in fact created by the NAM and was never independent.

powerful labor figure of the era. There were many reasons, discussed in studies of the CIO, for the decision of John L. Lewis and his chief aides in the Mine Workers to break away from the AFL and form the CIO.[9] The most significant single factor had nothing to do with ideology: John L. Lewis had been unable to crack the miners owned by the steel industry. Lewis first formed a Committee for Industrial Organization within the AFL to bring unionism into mass-production industries, including steel. As employers, the steel barons had successfully resisted unionism not only of their plant workers but also of those mining coal for the steel mills. They feared that organizing their miners would be an opening wedge for organizing their steelworkers. Big John L., on the other hand, fully understood, first, the historic commitment of the AFL chieftains to the concept of "exclusive jurisdiction" for various crafts and the inevitability of failure if unions again tried to organize unskilled mass-production workers on a craft basis; and second, the necessity of organizing captive miners to preserve organizational gains made in the rest of the coal industry by the United Mine Workers.

Thus, in addition to the AFL, there was in 1945 the new mass, open union movement represented by the CIO. The CIO was now a powerful force in basic manufacturing, claiming equality of status with the AFL for all domestic and international policy making. The successes of the CIO in the prewar years greatly enlarged the scope of unionism. One needs to recall, however, that despite their broader organizing base and acceptance of radicals during the organizing stages, CIO leaders shared with AFL leaders a simple but narrow objective: to create and sustain combinations of workers for purposes of collective bargaining in the existing economy, not to fundamentally alter ownership or management relations. In this respect, the two major labor federated bodies in the USA were acting out a leadership pattern that the Webbs found in their classic study of the British labor leaders. These men, Beatrice and Sidney Webb wrote, were "strong, self-reliant and pugnacious"; their "spirit" had brought them to the top in associations that were formed by "people [who] discover that they can do better for themselves by uniting to fight someone else than by opposing each other." But these very qualities, and the narrow objectives of the early unions, the Webbs observed, led most union leaders to become "Conservative" in a social sense, even if they were willing, when necessary, to lead strikes. Having achieved a degree of control over their own trades, with or without the use of the strike, these "Conservatives"

[9]American Federation of Labor, *History, Encyclopedia, Reference Book*, 3 vols. (Washington, D.C.: AFL, 1960), Vol. III, Part II, p. 2192.

maintained "a strong presumption in favour of the *status quo,*" "distrusted innovation," and had a liking for "distinct social classes." They favored a sort of feudal stability "based on each man being secured and contented in his station of life."[10]

The Wagner Act of 1935 declared the right of workers to organize, choose their own representatives, and bargain collectively with their employers. A National Labor Relations Board (NLRB) was given the authority to enforce the purposes of the act, including the authority to require employers to bargain and to prevent employers from specified "unfair labor practices" that would thwart organizing and collective bargaining. As noted by the first NLRB chairman, Judge J. Warren Madden, "for the first time the federal government was attempting to enforce widely its policy of outlawing employer interference with the right of workers to bargain collectively."[11]

Labor Fragmentation During the New Deal

The New Deal was generally friendly to unions, but labor solidarity was still rare. Indeed, the two major federations took divergent views even with respect to the National Labor Relations (Wagner) Act, then the basic labor law, as well as on the questions of political action. The CIO wanted to preserve and strengthen the Wagner Act and the powers of the National Labor Relations Board, and developed political action to preserve that act and its growing alliance with the New Deal. The AFL, on the other hand, had since 1935 been aligning itself with opponents of both. Temporarily departing from the sacred Gompers doctrine of neutrality, the Federation took a prominent role in hostile congressional investigations of the NLRB for alleged communist leanings. The AFL's own and more specific and direct motive for attacking the NLRB was the belief that it was showing "bias" against the older, predominantly craft-based AFL unions. The AFL subsequently decided that to protect its interests it should go beyond criticisms of the NLRB and sponsor amendments to the act and appropriations riders – again joining congressional opponents of the New Deal and the CIO – to enforce craft-based elections rather than the industrial-type bargaining units favored by the Roosevelt-appointed NLRB.

Legitimized by, and with considerable help from, the Wagner Act and the

---

[10]Sidney Webb and Beatrice Webb, *Industrial Democracy* (London: Longman, 1902), pp. 596–9 et passim.
[11]Harry A. Millis and Emily Clark Brown, *From the Wagner Act to Taft-Hartley* (Chicago: University of Chicago Press, 1950), pp. 29, 33. Millis died in 1948, after completing the planning of the book and much of the writing.

NLRB, most organized mass-production employees – in autos, electrical manufacturing, rubber, steel, and so on – were by 1937 working under contracts signed by unions affiliated with the CIO.

Labor's Vulnerability in World War II

In spite of substantial gains, the unions' political vulnerability was demonstrated in the midst of World War II. In 1943, Congress enacted the War Labor Disputes (Smith-Connally) Act over President Roosevelt's veto. That act, sponsored by two conservative Democrats, Representative Howard Smith (Va.) and Senator John Connally (Tex.), was supported by the NAM and business groups opposed to the unions and to the Wagner Act. Smith-Connally was a blunt warning that despite labor's voluntary wartime no-strike pledge, the New Deal Wagner Act, and the wartime temporary tripartite National War Labor Board, neither the employers nor Congress were ready to accept the new and strengthened status of labor. Smith-Connally may be seen also as a clear signal of Big Labor's continuing weakness in the political arena despite the friendly and Democratic White House, the CIO Political Action Committee, and wartime economic conditions, which favored union growth.

The War Labor Disputes Act was publicized as a means of stopping strikes, but one of the more lasting provisions of this otherwise temporary law was the one forbidding any union from making financial contributions to candidates in federal elections – a clear jab at the CIO PAC.

Although the Smith-Connally Act was repealed within six months of the end of the war, the ban on electoral contributions was incorporated in the new Labor Management Relations Act of 1947, popularly known as the Taft-Hartley Law.

Some important writers have viewed Smith-Connally as aimed mainly against John L. Lewis and the now independent United Mine Workers.[12] Lewis, having quit the CIO, was once again wielding great economic clout through his tight control of the strategically placed huge and rich United Mine Workers of America (UMWA). He had no use for the voluntary no-strike pledge taken by the AFL and the CIO. By striking the coalfields during the war, he could not only halt coal production in general but also, by extension, interrupt the operation of manufacturing, shipbuilding, and other plants as

[12]Arthur S. Link, *American Epoch: A History of the United States since the 1890's* (New York: Knopf, 1967), p. 536.

well. But in spite of his power, Lewis was a strong believer in capitalism and free market–based bargaining. My view is that the Smith-Connally Act was not aimed primarily at this Republican Party labor leader. Nor was it aimed at communists, who had been the publicized target of Representative Smith since the onset of the CIO and the Wagner Act. For Smith, the communists and the New Deal were inextricably related problems. But the political reality was that the Communist Party of the United States (CPUSA) and its wartime successor, the Communist Political Association (CPA), were among the most fervent of all supporters of the U.S. war effort after June 1941, and enforcers of the no-strike pledge. The CP-influenced unions generally continued to press for equal rights for blacks and for their fuller representation in union leadership. During the war, the communists were backing the bill for a permanent federal Fair Employment Practices Commission but were not pressing for broad social reform. While they were advocating peace, coexistence with the Soviet Union, the broad interests of the labor movement, labor unity, and support for the New Deal, communist labor leaders publicly deplored the Miners' strikes and generally despised Lewis, who was the most conspicuous strike leader of the era. The CP's attitude toward Lewis would, however, shift after he became the foremost labor union opponent of the Taft-Hartley Act, as is shown in Chapter 5.

The political clause of Smith-Connally was not directed at the American Federation of Labor, whose strategic leadership included about as many Republicans as Democrats. Except for its moves against the NLRB, the AFL had eschewed political action all through the New Deal years, in line with its ancient tradition.

Under Lewis, the Miners were achieving growth and membership gains by market-based bargaining, withholding labor as they saw fit but avoiding the political weaponry Lewis had initiated as the CIO's first president.

Thus, I conclude that the political provision of Smith-Connally, like the later Taft-Hartley Law, was mainly aimed at the CIO. The clause forbidding union contributions in federal elections was clearly aimed at that organization, which had been politically active since 1936, aiding liberal, "pro-labor," or "progressive" candidates of both major parties, mainly the Democrats; funds from CIO-affiliated union treasuries became important in campaigns for Roosevelt and Roosevelt supporters. Among the few unions that helped support the National Committee to Abolish the Poll Tax and early fights for racial equality, CIO-affiliated unions stood out. Not unexpectedly, such labor-sponsored politics were perceived as a threat by Smith and Connally, both from poll-tax states.

The CIO Political Action Committee (PAC)

The Smith-Connally Act of 1943 may have hastened the organization of the CIO Political Action Committee in 1943, but it was not its immediate cause. The chief threat that precipitated the PAC was the aftermath of the 1942 congressional elections, which alarmed virtually all key CIO leaders – center, left, and right – because it showed a resurgence of congressional opposition to union growth and to the New Deal. The revival of conservatism in 1942 lifted the hopes of such southern Democrats as Howard Smith and John Connally, who had been unhappy with the New Deal in general and the Wagner Act in particular. And the congressional loss in 1942 frightened Sidney Hillman and other centrist CIO leaders into a revival and expansion of full-time political action, mainly to preserve the New Deal legacy.

The CIO's Right Wing Resists PAC-Type Politics

Recognition of the need for defensive politics by the CIO seemed to transcend the factionalism in that organization. This was an illusion. The CIO was badly split, even though the highly publicized Political Action Committee had been founded by the CIO itself in 1943. And labor as a whole simply did not have the political organization required for success against the industrialists' unified plans and organization.

The AFL was still opposing both the CIO and its PAC idea. On the surface, the AFL had a community-based network of potential political activists in its "city centrals." Every major city had a delegate body representing AFL locals. Similar delegate councils existed in many counties and all the states. But while determined to be politically neutral and trying to keep the local councils from developing political independence, the national AFL, as well as the locals, had on occasion shown political muscle. Moreover, it was known that some city centrals had been in the forefront of independent political action in earlier periods. Also, as far back as 1906, AFL president Samuel Gompers, citing the British Trades Union Congress, formed a coalition of labor, farm, and progressive political organizations that threatened to go so far as to challenge the two-party system unless the legal status of unions was made secure.[13] Moreover, the AFL showed its political clout in 1931 when it succeeded in gaining enactment of the Davis-Bacon Act, which required all

[13]*Socialist Party Campaign Book* (Chicago, 1912) (in the author's personal collection).

contractors on federally financed construction to pay construction (mainly skilled) workers prevailing, usually union, wage rates.

During the war, AFL president William Green made the AFL presence felt at the war agencies and on Capitol Hill. The Federation membership swelled. Even in 1945, the national AFL and its construction unions were trying to protect and broaden Davis-Bacon, which many craft union leaders referred to as "*our* Wagner Act." The Federation had a veteran lobbyist to represent its interests on the Hill. Of course, many of the AFL officers and staff were aware of how much both the political economy of the United States and the labor force had changed since the days of Gompers. But as late as 1945, political neutralism remained the guiding philosophy of the Federation and put it in opposition to the CIO PAC.

The CIO had moved quickly in the late 1930s to form – alongside the AFL city centrals – its own industrial union councils (IUCS) at city, county, and state level. However, from my direct observation in New York, Buffalo, Detroit, Chicago, Los Angeles, and other cities in 1943–7, there was rarely more than token cooperation between the AFL city centrals and the CIO-affiliated IUCS. Moreover, replicating AFL city central leaders' practices, the CIO council leaders often made their connections and deals with local political bosses. For such dealings, the party tie of neither the CIO officer nor the political boss mattered much. Yet the CIO unionists in general were far more likely – but by no means certain – to reflect and reinforce the broad-based, pro-liberal pressure politics of the CIO Political Action Committee.

As PAC chairman, Sidney Hillman frequently complained privately of the lag between CIO official rhetoric and performance at the local, state, and national levels. When the PAC was created in 1943, there was no rush by CIO-affiliated "internationals" to sign up with seed money from their treasuries. Most, including the UAW, hesitated to create mechanisms for collecting the dollar-per-member voluntary contribution sought by the PAC for candidates in federal elections.

Partly because the two top UAW officers, President Thomas and Secretary-Treasurer Addes, were so obviously committed, but mainly because of my own convictions about the need for labor political action, I plunged into PAC-style political action, adding to my legislative function the title of UAW-CIO Director of Political Action. From this vantage point, I witnessed and helped direct the opening test of local union support, the 1943–4 voluntary financial collection from the membership for electoral campaigns. (Smith-Connally prohibited the use of treasury monies.) I received no support from Vice-

President Reuther and his staff, and very little support from "Reuther" locals, or from Reuther-controlled regional offices. As already indicated, the reason for this split was that factionalism generally superseded the external menace. On the other hand, Reuther was already building his own bridges to the Democrats in Michigan and elsewhere, and he would become an important figure in the national Democratic Party by 1948, after he became president of the UAW and had gained a majority on the international executive board of the union. He even risked antagonizing some on the left of his predominantly rightist UAW political coalition by pulling away from the Michigan Commonwealth Federation after having encouraged that third-party movement in 1943.[14]

Thomas and Addes still symbolized the left-center coalition, which in the CIO as well as in the UAW constituted the bedrock foundation for the CIO PAC. It was successful in mobilizing both union and nonunion support for the Roosevelt fourth-term campaign. But the right generally quietly abstained or openly resisted. Paradoxically, despite the left-right split over the PAC, the 1943–4 period was probably the high point of that left-center coalition in the CIO in general. The united front was then accepted by Hillman as PAC chairman and, with some subtle distancing, by Philip Murray as CIO president.

Reuther's anticommunist coalition building was another form of united front. It was beginning to penetrate the national CIO and was reaching a high point in the pivotal UAW. Although Reuther represented a broad spectrum, his UAW-based right-wing coalition was mainly based on anticommunism, as it was in the United Electrical Workers (UE) and other faction-ridden CIO affiliates.[15]

Looking back from the defeats of 1946 and 1947 as well as the cooler political climate of the present, it is relatively easy to see that the right wing of the CIO was taking a stand inconsistent with its own recent past and wholly incompatible with successful PAC-type politics. From its very start, the CIO had depended on many who were known to be members of, or sympathetic to, the Communist Party. When it undertook the CIO PAC, communist-led unions and CP-influenced staffers were prominently involved at every stage.

---

[14]Interview with Paul Silver, Detroit, January 1946. Silver was then an international representative on the staff of my boss, Vice-President Richard T. Leonard. Silver had in the past supported Reuther and had been active in the organizing efforts of the Michigan Commonwealth Federation.

[15]Ronald W. Schatz, *The Electrical Workers: A History of Labor at General Electric and Westinghouse, 1923–60* (Champaign: University of Illinois Press, 1983), pp. 97ff.

On the other hand, Sidney Hillman, an intimate of the Roosevelts, had been anticommunist throughout his union career. In his own union, the Amalgamated Clothing Workers, he had fought the CP and was no longer in danger of defeat from a left or left-center grouping. In this respect, he may have lacked the incentive for Red-baiting that his old Socialist Party comrade, Walter Reuther, faced in the Auto Workers. But above all that, he remained committed to the New Deal. He frequently stated to associates that he believed the CPUSA at that juncture was committed to the New Deal equally at home and abroad, not to revolution. Accordingly, he made use of CP talents and energies just as he and Lewis and Murray had done for the initial CIO organizing in the auto, steel, and other basic industries.[16]

The CIO, with six million members and a seemingly powerful political machinery, had the appearance of Big Labor, especially after its highly publicized PAC role in the Democrats' successful 1944 campaign. But the AFL in 1944, as in earlier CIO-initiated political efforts, canceled out CIO power in the political arena. The AFL was the largest federation; it repeatedly and proudly endorsed the House Committee on Un-American Activities (which had consistently targeted "Reds" in the CIO). Perhaps the most decisive single voice for political policy on the AFL executive council was that of Matthew Woll, the long-time first vice-president, who, according to Harold Laski's 1948 study *The American Democracy,* had "social views compared to which Mr. Winston Churchill's may not unfairly be termed Bolshevik."[17] Woll was, of course, opposed to the New Deal. Woll and his colleagues on the executive council hated Hillman with a passion. They rejected his political leadership role as they had rejected his defense and wartime roles, when he was widely viewed by the general public as the labor representative in government, playing a role comparable to Ernest Bevin's in Britain.

The AFL was confident of its own economic power. Like the CIO, it had

[16]See Archie Robinson, *George Meany and His Times* (New York: Simon & Schuster, 1981), p. 121. While Meany and much of the labor hierarchy despised him, Hillman was one of the most respected labor figures in the United States. He had close ties with top government liberals, professionals, and business leaders, but for many years he was considered at the AFL a bête noire, because he had pulled his clothing workers out of the AFL in 1914 and had been an architect of the CIO from its beginnings in 1935. Although he was for a while the top labor figure in the defense and war agencies, he had become for many the hated bête rouge. One could hear at private AFL gatherings in 1943 and later years: "No telling what that Jew Socialist might do next." The reference in 1943 was to the prominent role Hillman took in the CIO PAC on behalf of Roosevelt. In 1945, a year before Hillman's death, AFL officialdom was also angry about his influence in the arena of world labor organization on behalf of the CIO, heretofore an exclusive AFL preserve (discussed below).

[17]Harold J. Laski, *The American Democracy: A Commentary and an Interpretation* (New York: Viking, 1948), p. 131.

also spread into industrial-type workplaces. It was not interested in postwar progressive political coalitions. It came out of the war with a membership and resources that far surpassed the CIO's. But the Federation had a minimal agenda in Congress. Having won the Davis-Bacon Act under a Republican administration, it could feel vindicated for both its historical policy of political neutralism ("Reward your friends and punish your enemies," Gompers had said) and government-free, market-based unionism. Thus, unlike the CIO, the Federation showed no alarm when the president and Congress took early demobilization steps. The Federation welcomed the return to prewar normalcy.

The CIO, however, looking to the federal government for continued assistance, was still being friendly toward the White House. In a radio speech on October 30, 1945, President Truman heartened CIO leaders when he called for a general wage increase. In that address, he said a wage increase could be made with no major price changes. The CIO seized on that speech for its approach to postwar wage policy: a government-sponsored cost-of-living increase in wages. Immediately after the speech, Truman's new secretary of labor, Lewis Schwellenbach, under CIO prodding wrote a letter to Benjamin Fairless, president of U.S. Steel, asking him to discuss the wage issue with the CIO Steel Workers, indicating in his letter that a wage increase was in order: The company could afford it because the president had approved a steel price increase.[18]

When Murray received an invitation in August from President Truman to attend planning sessions for a voluntaristic labor-management conference to be held in November 1945, he continued to look for government aid. He tried to place on the agenda a proposal for a general wage increase. He offered this as an essential step toward the avoidance of industrial stoppages, the stated aim of the president's conference. Murray feared, as did Hillman, that the employers at this meeting would seek allies for their own determination to regain full control of the workplace and to reduce the bargaining power of the new unions in the CIO, by provoking strikes if necessary. Murray was also quite aware that the CIO was isolated from the labor invitees in seeking political support for postwar wage and legislative policies.

CIO staffers in Washington were equally alert to our need for aid from the White House and the opposition from other labor leaders. In a 1945 report I sent out to UAW-CIO and other labor sympathizers, I cautioned that the president's announced Labor-Management Conference "will in all likelihood

---

[18]U.S. Archives, Department of Labor, Secretary's files, box 174, "Labor Management" folder.

bog down," mainly on account of John L. Lewis' and William Green's rejection of CIO president Murray's attempt to place the question of a general wage increase on the agenda of the conference. I also noted what I regarded as the essentially political point Phil Murray and Sidney Hillman were stressing: "Management is planning strikes in the basic industries."[19] In short, we were reluctant to strike.

This fear, widely held in the CIO, was not shared by the AFL or the Miners. The unaffiliated, one-million-strong railroaders were not concerned. The Labor-Management Conference would once again demonstrate how dependent the CIO had become on continued government intervention. And by demonstrating that dependence, the conference also illustrated how fragmented the labor movement was at the end of World War II.

The CIO's Continued Reliance on Political Assistance

While the Truman administration in 1945 addressed the problem of reconversion, it gave mixed signals on the role it would play in labor-management relations in postwar America. In August 1945, within a few weeks of VJ-Day, the work of the tripartite National War Labor Board was terminated by President Truman's Executive Order 9599.

Unlike the AFL and the Miners, who were unshaken, CIO president Philip Murray lamented to the CIO executive board that, as a result of Executive Order 9599, a "complete vacuum" existed. Murray saw the CIO faced with an extremely serious challenge to its bargaining system: "There was nothing you could do with the Government, you were pushed right back to where you were before the war, ostensibly to take whatever action you thought was necessary to get what you were entitled to."[20] Murray said at the same meeting that all major CIO unions faced a "sit-down strike" by industry.

---

[19]Irving Richter, "Made in Washington," *Ammunition* (UAW-CIO monthly), 3, no. 12 (December 1945): 17. For a fuller discussion of the Labor-Management Conference, see Chapter 2.

[20]AFL-CIO Archives, CIO Executive Board, proceedings of meeting on November 1, 1945, p. 38. Philip Murray's pessimism about the opportunity to deal with employers after the War Labor Board ceased functioning reflected the historic reliance of the CIO on the state for aid in breaking the resistance of employers in basic industry as well as its continued dependence on the state during the war years. In this discussion, Murray, however, also outlined his own efforts to develop what he called a "concise" (CIO-wide) wage proposal to employers for the automobile, electrical manufacturing, rubber, and steel workers' unions – his euphemism for centralization in wage bargaining, an area heretofore left to each international in both the AFL and the CIO. This ambiguity is part of the CIO legacy as well as being indicative of Philip Murray's complex personality. The latter deserves far more exploration than this study provides.

The Management-Labor Charter

The minutes of the board meeting on November 1 show that Murray won unanimous approval for this view of industrialists being on a strike of their own. To offset what he considered an industry postwar legislative offensive, he had also won approval at an earlier board meeting for a "Management-Labor Charter," or status-quo agreement, which the CIO drafted in the spring of 1945. The CIO hoped top union and top management would sign the charter and thereby head off the growing threats of congressional legislation to reverse the Wagner Act, the New Deal's keystone labor law.

In sum, the CIO, unlike the AFL and the Miners, approached the issue of postwar labor relations with an essentially political, albeit defensive, outlook. But this position did not have unanimous support. Murray's own approach was ambivalent. He knew strikes were inevitable but feared them. He was also reluctant to see Walter Reuther, already a major figure in the developing economic and political confrontations between labor and capital, take leadership of the General Motors strike called in November 1945. Reuther did not appear among the delegates chosen by Murray to represent the CIO at the Labor-Management Conference. He was also wholly ignored by Murray's staff in the preparation of the earlier CIO-initiated Management-Labor Charter. While Murray questioned Reuther's taking the GM workers out on strike (at about the time that the Labor-Management Conference convened), Reuther's leadership of that first big postwar strike is widely believed to have been decisive for his election to the UAW presidency in 1946 (an event that helped shift Murray to the right) and for his subsequent rise to the presidency of the entire CIO in 1952, when he succeeded Murray.

Reuther's leadership of the GM action demonstrated that he could lead a successful national strike, but the record is unclear about his own postwar policy. Despite a wide belief that he symbolized industrial militancy, there is evidence that Reuther had agreed to taking a Hillman-Murray approach shortly before the GM strike; namely, that a strike could be prevented and the wage issue settled by a government-sponsored agreement. Reuther was in 1945 not only director of the General Motors Department but responsible also for price-consumer functions, directly managed by Donald E. Montgomery of the UAW Washington office. Montgomery was a ghostwriter for, and a close adviser of, Reuther on relations with the national CIO as well as on all wage matters. Joseph Goulden reports that Reuther and Montgomery, as well as Phil Murray, William Green, and Eric Johnston, president of the Chamber of

Commerce of the United States, were all approached in early 1945 by Chester Bowles, newly appointed director of the Truman administration's Office of Price and Wage Stabilization, for a combined deal that would give workers a general 10 percent wage increase in return for a one-year postwar no-strike pledge. According to this account, all of the parties agreed to Bowles' proposition, but the plan was nixed by President Truman and Secretary of Labor Schwellenbach because they thought there was not the inflation danger that Bowles feared.[21]

The CIO's political strategy, designed to head off the growing tide of antilabor bills in Congress, seemed to be partially successful when both AFL president William Green and the Chamber president, Eric Johnston, agreed to sign the CIO-initiated charter early in 1945. However, this turned out to be a paper victory. When the president's Labor-Management Conference convened in November of 1945, the Chamber and the National Association of Manufacturers showed a solid united front for their own political objective: to roll back union power. AFL president Green also moved away, going over to the market-based view argued by John L. Lewis. In contemptuous opposition to Murray's views, Lewis insisted on the resumption of a "free" economy. He saw the CIO's demand for a general wage increase as a political ploy to make up for the CIO's weak position vis-à-vis employers. At that historic tripartite meeting, which I will discuss in more detail in the next chapter, the three chiefs of organized labor – Green, Lewis, and Murray – showed hostility to each other bordering on farce. Organized business, by contrast, exhibited solidarity. With one voice it made clear to the country that the business community was ready to limit collective bargaining by entering the legislative and political arenas. Its unified objective was to roll back labor gains achieved by workers during the New Deal and during the war.

The Strike Wave of 1945–6

The CIO-sponsored charter failed. The president's conference also failed. Following the failures of both, the unions participated in a record-breaking strike wave that peaked in mid 1946. But while these strikes may have saved

---

[21]Joseph Goulden, *The Best Years: 1945–1960* (New York: Atheneum, 1976), pp. 115–16. Goulden was in later years a confidant of labor leaders. He was even commissioned by AFL-CIO president George Meany to write a definitive biography of Meany and was given full access to AFL and CIO papers, but Meany, unhappy with the book, ordered a new authorized biography by Archie Robinson (see n. 16) based mainly on Meany's taped recollections.

bargaining systems and gained many wage increases, labor failed to stop a consequent victory at the polls by the Republican Party in 1946 and a resulting anti-union, anti–New Deal backlash in the Congress that convened in 1947.

Economic change by itself could have produced a strike movement as the Second World War neared its end, as it did after World War I. However, experts and politicians now saw the change from a perspective of fear. Sumner Slichter feared that "a laboristic society" was already succeeding the "capitalistic one."[22]

We have seen that by 1944 and 1945 the National Association of Manufacturers, designated as the voice of American industry at the very beginning of the New Deal, was mounting a counterrevolution in preparation for postwar labor relations. Its fundamental purpose was to weaken the gains made by various unions over the years, especially after the advent of the CIO and the National Labor Relations (Wagner) Act. The NAM made publicly clear its position at two voluntaristic events in 1945: the Management-Labor Charter devised by the CIO to maintain existing New Deal labor law and the president's Labor-Management Conference.[23]

The analysis of these two events in the next chapter illuminates the NAM's methods and goals as well as the conflicting postwar approaches of the major union centers at this beginning of a turning point in U.S. labor history.

[22]*Trade Unions in a Free Society,* p. 71.

[23]For an influential and more demonic view, see Henry Pelling, *American Labor* (Chicago: University of Chicago Press, 1960). Although Pelling is best known as a historian of British labor, his small one-volume American labor history has been an influential part of the University of Chicago series "American Civilization," edited by Daniel Boorstin. Representative of a younger generation of scholars writing on the period are Harvey A. Levenstein, *Communism, Anticommunism and the CIO* (1981), and Schatz, *The Electrical Workers.* For a more general history up to 1984, see Ronald L. Filipelli, *Labor in the USA* (1984), which gives a good account of some of the events of this period as well as integrating those events with later developments in labor-management relations.

2

SEARCHING FOR COEXISTENCE: THE MANAGEMENT-LABOR CHARTER AND THE LABOR-MANAGEMENT CONFERENCE

Two major voluntaristic efforts were made in 1945 to reach a labor and management agreement for the postwar years, one of which, the president's Labor-Management Conference held in November and December, has received significant notice.[1] The present study will revisit and reinterpret that important event. To understand labor and management attitudes when that conference was convened, the generally neglected Management-Labor Charter, initiated by the CIO six months earlier, is highly relevant for a grasp of the "labor problem" circa 1945–50.

Labor unrest, endemic in all modern industrial societies, was a great public concern in the United States in the final months of the Second World War. All three major labor centers – the AFL, the CIO, and the railroad brotherhoods – participated in a record-breaking wave of strikes. There was special public anxiety, however, about the spreading CIO-led strikes in the basic industries. By their very nature, these stoppages involved masses of workers and more deeply affected the general public than the typical craft-based stoppages of the traditional AFL unions. In addition, the newly created industrial union movement still contained many figures on the left. All – left, center, and right – were now marching behind Philip Murray, the ex-miner who had succeeded John L. Lewis and carried the banner of the Congress of Industrial Organizations. The policies of the politically moderate Murray were ambiguous. His devotion to the institution was unequivocal. He had a genuine fear, however, shared by most of his members in 1945, about the ability of the CIO to survive in the postwar era.

---

[1]"The conference demonstrated for the first time in history that at a national level representatives from both labor and management could meet together without arguing as to whether or not collective bargaining was desirable." (Arthur F. McClure, *The Truman Administration and the Problems of Postwar Labor, 1945–1948* [Cranbury, N.J.: Associated University Presses, 1969], p. 63).

CIO Objectives in 1945

To understand Murray's promotion of the conciliatory Management-Labor Charter idea, one should recall that the CIO was helped initially (in the mid 1930s) by a friendly White House, that a labor law and labor board approved by the president legitimized collective bargaining for all workers, and that conditions of full employment and continued full legality during the war helped sustain the new labor body. The CIO's great fear as the war neared its end was that employers would launch an offensive against them to weaken if not wipe out their still vulnerable movement.

But Murray was not free of bureaucratic concerns. While he was convinced that organized employers in basic industry wanted a showdown, he also sought to obtain centralized control over member unions. To preserve his prestige and friendships in government as well as to demonstrate patriotism, he wanted to maintain the wartime no-strike pledge, which in turn would assure a return to the prewar legal status, which included the right to strike, and continued protection by government. To accomplish these goals, the CIO's president needed to control or coordinate strikes as well as guarantee continuation of the Wagner Act.

The AFL and the CIO both supported the wartime voluntary no-strike pledge given Roosevelt immediately after Pearl Harbor. The strikes that did occur were considered either "unofficial" or "wildcat," with the notable exception of those led by John L. Lewis of the Mine Workers, the then unaffiliated union. Lewis was ready to continue to challenge the government and the operators in the postwar era. The American Federation of Labor, with which Lewis was ready to reaffiliate the Miners, followed a somewhat more ambiguous line, but was also planning to return to traditional market-based "business" unionism after the war.

Murray left no doubt about his real commitment to the pledge during wartime. Viewing the mounting wave of union-instigated stoppages when the war was nearing an end in 1944–5, his main concern seemed to be that strikes were playing into the hands of industry leaders opposed to the CIO. In January 1944, he talked to his executive board about having given his "sacred" word to President Roosevelt to retain the pledge, while at the same time warning the CIO board that industry was provoking most of the strikes in basic industry in order to repeal the Wagner Act and undermine any government policies that might assist unions. After indicating his fears, he hinted that postwar strikes might have to be curbed voluntarily in order to thwart industry plans.

Though fully aware of internal splits, Murray was not yet taking sides. He knew, as did all CIO leaders, that in 1944 the pivotal Auto Workers affiliate was engaged in its as yet sub-rosa factional struggle over whether to continue the no-strike pledge, which had become an indirect test of Walter Reuther's challenge of the incumbent president, R. J. Thomas. Murray had won the official backing of all affiliated unions for continuation of the pledge. As the unrest seethed in all industries beneath formal adherence to the no-strike pledge, he described to the CIO board his own efforts, as the Steel Workers' negotiator, to avoid strikes by seeking settlements at the National War Labor Board (NWLB). "You can't win a strike these days . . . while the war is on," he told the CIO board. With a strong hint of what might be facing the CIO negotiators in the postwar period, he added, "Three quarters of the estimated stoppages in the past year [in steel] . . . were provoked by employers." He even told how he had led a back-to-work action in some steel locals and had fired a staff representative of that international union for "threatening to strike" a steel plant.[2]

Murray was vehement about supporting continuation of the no-strike pledge, in part because he was hoping that if he could not personally coordinate postwar CIO wage policy, he would at least set a pattern in steel, where he bossed the United Steel Workers; other CIO unions would then follow the steel pattern. While such personal interests were not expressed by Murray publicly, I often heard this preference expressed informally by R. J. Thomas, Murray's closest ally on the CIO board. It was well known that in the UAW-CIO, factional considerations – present in virtually all issues – entered into the calculation of not only Murray but also Thomas and George F. Addes, the strongman of the Addes-Thomas UAW caucus. Both men knew that success in holding off the first postwar strikes would have the effect of warding off the national strike at General Motors that Reuther, as director of the UAW's General Motors Department, could stage. If such a strike were successful, it would greatly enhance the challenge of "the Redhead" for the UAW-CIO presidency and thereby upset the delicate balance in the auto union and the entire CIO. It would also upstage Murray and in his view be used by industry for its own postwar plans to reverse the labor law.

Whatever the internal politics and unrest in 1944, Murray clearly was alarmed by the strike picture in early 1945. The total number of strikes for 1945, already unfolding before VJ-Day, would reach four thousand and break the standing record of 38 million man-days idle.[3] An important internal politi-

---

[2]CIO Executive Board, minutes, January 18, 1944, pp. 217–28.
[3]U.S. Department of Commerce, Bureau of the Census, *Historical Statistics of the United States, 1789–1945* (Washington, D.C.: Government Printing Office, 1949), p. 73.

cal point to note here is that in response to Murray's plea, the CIO board at the January 18 meeting suppressed its differences and voted unanimously for a resolution calling on all affiliates "to religiously and meticulously respect the sacred obligation" of the wartime pledge by "avoiding any stoppages of work or interruption of production."

The Management-Labor Charter

It was against this complicated background that the CIO drafted a Management-Labor Charter. Clearly designed to avoid or minimize strike action and preserve the legislative status quo, it was presented to the top labor and management leaders in March 1945. After approval from Murray for the general idea, the charter was drafted in the office of Dr. Robert K. Lamb, national legislative representative of the United Steel Workers (USW-CIO), by Lamb and his assistant, Edith Pratt.[4] Lamb had sensitive political antennae. He understood Murray. He knew the factional alignments. He first secured informal approval from middle-of-the-road and right-wing representative officers of the CIO before taking the draft to Murray for his approval.[5] The statement was quickly signed by Murray. Murray in turn was able to get the signature of his own former Miners Union colleague, AFL president William Green. Lamb got the signature and cooperation of Eric Johnston, president of the Chamber of Commerce of the United States. Lamb, formerly an economist on the staffs of various U.S. government agencies, was quite aware that the Chamber had been a creature of the National Association of Manufacturers. But he and other CIO staffers and officers felt that Johnston personally would agree to coexistence. Lamb, operating with Murray's approval, had enjoyed a close association with Johnston during the war, outside the NAM orbit. Johnston was one of a group of corporate executives then creating the Committee for Economic Development (CED). The CED, in turn, had attracted not only CIO but also AFL support, at least at the staff level.

Many trusted staffers considered the new business organization a gathering point for "progressive" capitalists – an offset, they hoped, to the historically anti-union NAM and its affiliated employer associations. Officers as well as

---

[4]This view is directly contradicted by Howell John Harris, who attributes the authorship of the charter to Eric Johnston, president of the Chamber of Commerce of the United States (*The Right to Manage: Industrial Relations Policies of American Business* [Madison: University of Wisconsin Press, 1982], p. 110).

[5]Letter from Edith Pratt to the author, March 4, 1984.

staffers of the CIO and some AFL staffers attended early CED meetings and met with Johnston and other individual members and prospective member firms' officers during the war. The CIO attenders believed that these employers not only tolerated unions and existing labor law but were committed to winning the war and stood for expanded employment and trade after the war – all CIO hopes as well.

Thus, while Lamb and other CIO staffers in Washington were aware of the Chamber's ties to the NAM – and that Johnston as president of the Chamber was not really representative of the vast Chamber organization – we helped promote the notion that Johnston's signature on the agreement would help dissuade Congress from weakening the labor law. We feared the NAM-led employers' political and industrial power. Although we often expressed great faith in the potential power of labor, in CIO-type mass unions, in Murray's leadership, and in the Wagner Act as a legitimizing factor, we were in actuality uncertain about our survival after the war. We could, therefore, easily rationalize the muting of strikes during the reconversion period. What we did not realize is that even many of those we considered to be "progressive" capitalists would be swayed by the thrust of organized employer associations against existing labor law and against the existing power of unions.

Eric Johnston did sign the charter as president of the Chamber of Commerce of the United States. However, before the year was over, Johnston moved to the side of the NAM president, Ira Mosher, in a united front against the entire, badly fractured, labor delegation at the president's Labor-Management Conference in November-December 1945.

Even as Eric Johnston signed the charter, he stipulated that he was doing so "subject to the approval" of the organization he represented. That condition was never met, so far as Chamber records indicate. William Green, who also signed as president of the American Federation of Labor, made no such stipulation; but his signing was made into a nonevent by the AFL. John L. Lewis flatly refused to sign. Only the CIO, of the major labor organizations, signed and ratified the signing.

The CIO was showing an extremely conciliatory approach to labor-management relations. First, the very wording of the title of the charter – Management-Labor Charter – was a reversal of the usual language and had been deliberately chosen to suggest Labor deference to management authority. Second, the CIO drafters and principals agreed in advance to a basic demand then being put forward by the employer side, stating a joint acceptance of the principle that management had the "inherent right . . . to direct the operations of an enterprise."

The CIO drafters of the agreement emphasized in both the first and final clauses a concern labor ostensibly shared with management: an expanded economy after "complete victory over Nazism and Japanese militarism," as well as the major stipulation sought by Murray and the CIO, joint acceptance by labor and capital of the legislative status quo: the "fundamental rights of labor to organize and engage in collective bargaining . . . free from legislative enactments which would interfere with or discourage these objectives." As a quid pro quo for this legislative "victory," the CIO would accept the specific right of managers to manage – an issue that proved to be more thorny at the conference called later in 1945 by President Truman.

Given his own prestige and personal authority among all factions, Philip Murray had no problem getting approval from the CIO board with only a single qualification, from an ex-socialist turned right-wing leader, George Baldenzi of the United Textile Workers. Baldenzi would not accept the words "free enterprise." The two words were removed after he uttered distaste for the "constant repetition" of them. "It doesn't smell very good," Baldenzi said. There is no other recorded objection from a CIO executive board member.[6] After Murray, Green, and Johnston signed and the charter received unanimous approval from the CIO executive board, the *CIO News* proclaimed, "It's Industrial Peace for the Postwar Period" in a three-column headline.[7]

The CIO's national executive board on April 12, 1945, proclaimed:

[The Board] wholeheartedly approves this Charter and authorizes President Murray and the other representatives to serve on the national committee which is to be established under this Charter to participate in its work and seek to accomplish a full implementation of the principles set forth in the Charter.[8]

The board also rubber-stamped Murray's choices for the CIO representatives to join him for follow-up meetings: Sidney Hillman and R. J. Thomas, centrist presidents respectively of the Amalgamated Clothing Workers (ACW) and the United Auto Workers (UAW).

The fact that Murray omitted Reuther from the delegation to the Labor-Management Conference and assigned to Lamb major responsibility for the Management-Labor Charter merits some comment. Murray was thereby representing the united-front alignment that still prevailed at the CIO in 1945. There were still left-led internationals. On the national staff, Lee Pressman, with whom Murray and Lamb both worked, was general counsel. Len de

[6]CIO Executive Board, minutes, April 12, 1945, p. 38. The unanimity point is historically important, contradicting some well-known beliefs that only "the commies" were behind the charter.
[7]*CIO News*, April 2, 1945, p. 1.
[8]Minutes, April 12, 1945, p. 5.

Caux was publicity director. Both Pressman and de Caux, and their staffs, were considered members of the CP or sympathetic to it. Lamb's assignment probably reflected the importance attached to political action in general and underscored as well left-center continuity at the CIO in early 1945. Why didn't Murray choose for the assignment Nathan Cowan, who, with the title of CIO national legislative representative, would have appeared to be a logical choice? Cowan was an old comrade from the United Mine Workers, a reliable ally, and a pal of Murray's. He was to be one of the survivors on the staff after late 1947, when the CIO president began to switch away from his former united-front position and purge the left. As will be seen, by 1947 Murray and other labor leaders were reflecting and helping to change the political climate.

On the technical side, Murray knew that Cowan's skills were limited; that he could not be relied upon for such complexities as drafting documents or identifying personalities and interests among the disparate employer associations in industries outside coal mining. Lamb, on the other hand, was a poised former professor of economics, a trained researcher with excellent connections. As for political considerations, Lamb was close to, but not of, the left. The Murray-CIO stance required knowledgeable, competent, and skilled staffers for the delicate, hold-the-line, status-quo position the CIO was pursuing. But in addition Lamb was a practical choice for the internal, Murray-led, left-center coalition. Lamb occupied a point somewhere between center and left on the ideological spectrum, able to work with both, and with many on the right too. But he was also loyal to Murray; he was discreet, yet knew how to flatter the CIO president.

Officially, Lamb represented the United Steel Workers-CIO and was on their payroll. But he cast a wider net during this united-front honeymoon era and had Murray's backing. In his monthly report for March 1945, "Report on Legislation," he did not confine himself to Steel Workers' matters. Lamb hailed the charter as "a great sign for organized labor," described Murray's charter role as a sign of his (Murray's) being one of "labor's statesmen," and expressed the central and immediate political hope of Murray and the CIO that "this meeting of minds between management and labor" would affect the attitude of Congress toward postwar labor legislation:

Although the war news crowded it quickly off the front pages of most newspapers, the signing of the new Labor Management Charter by President Murray of the CIO, President Green of the AFL, and Eric Johnston, President of the U.S. Chamber of Commerce, is of great significance for all of organized labor. It holds out the definite promise that in the postwar years, the cooperation of management and labor to win the war will be continued to win prosperity for the country. Many industrialists are recognizing that they have a common interest with organized labor in raising living standards, eliminating industrial strife, and creating a better life for the whole community, and labor's statesmen are overlooking their differences for the sake of working jointly for a better future.

It is to be expected that legislation in Congress will begin to reflect this meeting of minds between management and labor.[9]

As will be seen, none of this optimism at the CIO was warranted. Getting Johnston's signature turned out to be another paper victory, not an accurate barometer of industry's short-run or long-run intentions.

There was another prized paper victory for Bob Lamb and his staff, and for left and center people associated with the charter, the war effort, postwar peace plans, and hopes for a continuation of the Soviet-American wartime alliance. This hollow victory was the charter language in Clause 7:

An enduring peace must be secured. This calls for the establishment of an international security organization, with full participation by all the United Nations, capable of preventing aggression and assuring lasting peace.[10]

Neither John L. Lewis of the United Mine Workers nor Ira Mosher, president of the National Association of Manufacturers, agreed to sign the charter. Even Johnston's own organization, the Chamber of Commerce, did not endorse his signing, despite prominent press notice given to the document and a mimeographed twelve-page digest of press excerpts about the charter issued by the Chamber. The Chamber of Commerce copy of the agreement (printed) contains a vital qualifying clause absent from the mimeographed AFL copy: "subject to the approval of the three organizations."

The Chamber's librarian indirectly confirmed the institution's de facto nullification. She reported to me in 1979 that the Chamber's national office files contained nothing beyond its printed copy with the qualification noted and the previously mentioned digest of newspaper clippings about the charter.[11]

In its anxiety to show employer acceptance, the CIO clearly inflated the

---

[9]Murray papers, Catholic University of America, Box 12 (emphasis added). This memo is undated, except for the March reference, but it carries the stamped date of April 15, 1945, designating the date it was received by Murray's office.

[10]All charter quotations are taken from a copy found in the AFL-CIO library and now in my possession.

[11]A note, signed "Rose Racine, Chamber Librarian," appears on the bottom of my own original letter, dated April 20, 1979, which I sent to the Chamber to confirm a telephoned request for correspondence and other documents relating to the Chamber's and Johnston's activities regarding the charter. Ms. Racine enclosed the two documents cited above and added at the bottom of my letter: "Thank you for your inquiry. The enclosed pages [text of agreement and press excerpts] are the only material available about the agreement made between the Chamber and AFL and CIO. I hope this will be of help to you." This note was handwritten. No officer responded to my inquiry.

importance of Johnston's signing. For those who in early 1945 read newspaper reports of the Chamber's president agreeing to accept the status quo, it might have appeared that industrial peace was as imminent as the ending of the war itself. Even well-informed staffers, including me, who as representative of the UAW-CIO worked closely with Lamb and his assistant, chose to ignore the qualification inserted by President Johnston as well as Chamber tendencies contrary to labor. We ignored mentioning that the Chamber of Commerce had never accepted the New Deal or the New Deal labor laws. Indeed, the Chamber was possibly already preparing, and in any event would soon issue, new and inflammatory pamphlets on "Communism" and "Socialism," fashionable language for political activists on the right bent on undermining social reforms.

We also chose to overlook distinctly hostile propaganda the Chamber had circulated against the Wagner Act during the war, in 1944. Ironically, one such article was signed by Chamber president Johnston himself, though distributed by Ralph Bradford, the general manager. Entitled "Your Stake in Capitalism" and appearing in the popular arch-conservative magazine *Reader's Digest,* this article was sent to local Chambers and others by Bradford to generate support for what he said was the Chamber's mission, gaining "Public Support for Free Enterprise."

In short, the Chamber was showing its members that in the volatile period following the war's end it was advancing the interests of its members at the local, state, and national level. One of the probable outcomes of such grassroots political work was the adoption of state right-to-work laws, which helped pave the way for the Taft-Hartley Act of 1947. While all this political activity was bearing fruit for employers, labor leaders were keeping to traditional or "free" bargaining, or deluding themselves about support from business personalities.

While Johnston was the elected and temporary president of the Chamber, Bradford was managing head of the organization. It was he who maintained contacts with local Chamber managers and committees. In Bradford's own 1944 "ACTION" booklet, he gave the Chamber organizations in the states and cities a message wholly in accord with contemporary corporate politics. Congress, Bradford wrote, was the "'Fortress of Freedom' standing against the Federal bureaucracy." All business people recognized these code words; translated, they meant an end to wartime regulations and emasculation of New Deal labor laws.[12]

---

[12]Chamber of Commerce of the United States, *Congress Looks to Business: ACTION Suggestions for Chamber of Commerce LEADERSHIP in National Affairs* (pamphlet) (Washington, D.C., 1944), pp. 17, 5–6.

Through General Manager Ralph Bradford, the Chamber network was advised to nullify, not accept, existing law or existing bargaining relationships. In short, while the CIO-sponsored Management-Labor Charter may have been important for the CIO, it never was an operative position for the Chamber of Commerce of the United States.

In a public relations sense, Johnston's signing for the Chamber seemed to us the big catch. It is clear now we really netted only a minnow, and even that minnow soon got away.

The real leader of industry for labor affairs, the National Association of Manufacturers, never even nibbled at the bait. The NAM, soon to emerge as an architect of Taft-Hartley, was known on Capital Hill as a long-time opponent of unionism in any form. While it seemed to accept labor leaders and collective bargaining at the president's conference in 1945, the NAM was also financing and directing campaigns in the states for right-to-work legislation. Writing as the UAW-CIO legislative representative, I told our own members in reports and newsletters, and members of Congress in conversations, that the manufacturers' association was active on its own behalf and was sponsoring front organizations that carried the NAM message without the NAM imprint. During my rounds of congressional offices early in 1945, I often picked up, or was given by members, samples of NAM-initiated, sometimes NAM-sponsored, literature, all having a common political message: that unions were too powerful, that the pendulum had swung too far and should be brought back to curb labor and to give equal treatment to management and labor. Similar literature was handed out to UAW delegates visiting some members of Congress.[13]

By early 1945, it is true, labor's position had improved beyond the open-shop era. Industry had been forced, by spontaneous worker revolts and governmental action, to accept collective bargaining. Even in the basic mass-production industries, employers no longer wielded the unlimited power they had previously enjoyed. Many had been forced to sign contracts that took some control out of their hands and granted limited but real forms of industrial democracy. The NAM wanted none of this in the postwar United States. It had long favored an open shop, with no unions interfering. Although many NAM-

---

[13]One pamphlet, *Join the CIO and Build a Soviet America*, by Joseph Kamp, was given by Clare Hoffman (R., Mich.) to a UAW delegation from his home district. This pamphlet had been used extensively against the CIO in its 1936–40 organizing drives. Ostensibly published by the Committee for Constitutional Government, it was usually attributed by CIO organizers and publicists to the NAM.

led firms had signed union contracts before and during the war, there still was no official or de facto acceptance of unionism by the NAM as a whole or by its members, its affiliates, or its fronts.

The AFL's Withdrawal from the Charter

The American Federation of Labor, once again the largest and now somewhat broadened labor body, was still dominated by exclusionist craft-type affiliates. It looked with suspicion on any CIO-initiated political moves. The Federation was far from reconciled to coexistence with its brothers in the CIO and to mass, open unionism. Although President Green had joined Murray and signed the charter, the AFL explicitly underscored its ongoing conflict with the CIO when its delegation at the Labor-Management Conference broke with the CIO leadership on postwar wage policy. At that meeting, Green moved to the side of John L. Lewis and, indirectly, to the position favored by the NAM. In the context of the period, this preference of Lewis and Green for the continuation of traditional business unionism was as rational as Murray's peace plan, but it also conformed not with labor's but with industry's political strategy.

As for the Management-Labor Charter, despite Green's signature, his apparent agreement with Murray, and the brief flurry of AFL publicity in its support, the Federation seems to have converted it into a nonevent. The three-volume *History, Encyclopedia, Reference Book,* prepared for the Federation by George Meany while as AFL secretary-treasurer he was in charge of such matters, and published by the AFL in 1955 (three years after Meany became president), is based on "the most historically important subjects considered by the American Federation of Labor conventions." This work not only omits mention of the charter but, as if to emphasize the omission, cites numerous other labor-related events of 1945 under the heading "An Epochal Year – 1945." But the charter signed by Green and witnessed by Meany, and even publicized at an AFL-sponsored press conference in 1945, is not even mentioned.

AFL leaders David Dubinsky and Matthew Woll and their staffs were already advancing their own foreign-relief and foreign-affairs organizations. As for Meany, he was young, willing, and very able. He told his biographer, Archie Robinson, that he latched onto this field of AFL activity both because of his own interests and because he wanted to carve out for himself an area of union activity that was not already preempted by the AFL president, the aging

William Green.[14] In doing so, however, Meany found himself in conflict with the upstart CIO's claims for equality of status in the international arena.

This point requires a brief historical digression, one that may help illuminate the AFL's dissociation from the CIO on both foreign policy and labor policy and may cast new light on the CIO's motivation in the murky field of international relations circa 1945.

The AFL from the time of Gompers had maintained organizational ties with labor movements abroad. After World War I, labor federations of the Allied powers created an International Federation of Trade Unions (IFTU). The AFL had briefly joined and then quit the IFTU on account of what the executive council saw as socialist ideology.[15] But by the time Hitler came to power, and at about the time the CIO was being formed, the AFL, already deeply involved and competing with leaders of the CIO and some nationalists and leftists in Latin America, began to reconsider its position with respect to the International Federation. It rejoined the IFTU, citing the fact that its general secretary "maintained the closest relations with the [AFL-selected] workers' group of the governing body of the International Labor Organization (ILO) and the workers delegates to international labor conferences." The 1938 convention of the American Federation of Labor endorsed the decision of the executive council. Its carefully worded resolution pointed to: (1) the rise of Nazism in Germany; (2) the threat of war; (3) the persuasive conversations held by the executive council with Sir Walter Citrine, the moderate general secretary of the British Trades Union Congress (TUC); and finally, the cooperation between the IFTU and the ILO.[16]

This prewar action of the AFL left the CIO on the outside and the AFL very much on the inside of international labor organization as of the end of 1945.

Labor in the United States accepted the idea of the United Nations, and with the UN a continuation of the ILO. But there was as serious a division within labor unions on this phase of international politics as on domestic politics. Instead of making a joint approach, the American Federation of Labor and the Congress of Industrial Organizations each pursued its institutional interests. Prestige proved to be more important to the top leaders than international solidarity. While the AFL was largely satisfied with the exclusive representation it enjoyed at both the International Federation of Trade Unions and the

---

[14]*George Meany and His Times* (New York: Simon & Schuster, 1981), pp. 121ff.
[15]American Federation of Labor, *History, Enclycopedia, Reference Book*, 3 vols. (Washington, D.C.: AFL, 1960), Vol. II, Part I, pp. 1103–9.
[16]Ibid., pp. 1110–13.

ILO – in both cases it was the sole U.S. labor organization getting official international recognition – the CIO in these instances of international postwar arrangements was rejecting the status quo.

The prewar competition between the AFL and the CIO for representation in international organizations continued in the final months of the war. President Roosevelt's death on April 12, 1945, brought the matter to the surface, aggravating old conflicts. Immediately after Roosevelt's death the CIO moved quickly to protect its ILO position. Within a few weeks of Truman's accession to the presidency, Phil Murray called on him at the White House. Murray's purpose for this visit was solely to renew the CIO's previously declared claim to equal status on the governing board and at official meetings of the ILO. Murray's follow-up letter to President Truman included a summary of the CIO's efforts to have President Roosevelt's secretary of labor certify the CIO for official participation as an American labor center at the prewar ILO. Murray recalled for Truman that the CIO had temporarily withdrawn its demand during the war for "equality of representation with the American Federation of Labor" only "in order not to add to the burdens of the commander-in-chief," and had made the withdrawal "without prejudice" to the claim. There was a further stipulation in that arrangement with Roosevelt, Murray reminded Truman: namely, that the AFL delegate "will in no way speak for or represent the point of view of the Congress of Industrial Organizations."[17]

In reviving this divisive issue, Murray not only personally visited Truman at the White House but also wrote the new Truman-appointed secretary of labor, Lewis B. Schwellenbach, apprising him of the CIO stand vis-à-vis the AFL. Murray again asked for equal representation. Referring to the evolving International Security Organization, which became the United Nations, Murray declared to Truman and to Schwellenbach that "it becomes more important than ever that the request of the CIO, firmly grounded on merit and equality, should be granted."[18]

This digression suggests that the dynamics of competing labor politics in 1945 spilled over into the field of international affairs as each group prepared to advance its postwar agenda and protect its own status. The differences were not simply ideological, as many believed. Although some CIO individuals had their own ideological alignments and played a part in the CIO's move to

[17]U.S. Archives, Department of Labor, Secretary's files, box 174, "ILO" folder.
[18]Ibid. Copies of the 1944 exchange with Roosevelt were included in the letters sent by Murray to both Truman and Schwellenbach.

help form the World Federation of Trade Unions (WFTU), the major considerations for CIO president Murray in furthering the WFTU – and he was the decisive voice at CIO – appear to have been prestige and status.

Murray would open his split with the left in 1946. But in 1945 he helped create the WFTU as an international labor organization that embraced the CIO, the Soviet bloc, and communist-influenced labor confederations in Italy and France despite his personal and deeply held conservative views. In creating the WFTU, Murray was also probably influenced by the favorable view of it taken by CIO vice-president Hillman and by Sir Walter Citrine, the highly respected and very cautious general secretary of the British TUC, the latter of whom had been working with the Soviets since 1941. My own speculation is that Murray was looking for respectable approval of his own decision – initiated and approved by Hillman and the CP-left – to stake out an area in which the CIO was not frozen out by AFL preemption.

It adds to the ambiguities of this phase of labor politics to recall that while Murray was in 1945 still accepting left-wing support, he was also under the influence of the strongly anti-Soviet Catholic hierarchy in the United States.[19] Catholic prelates adorned the platforms of and sat in at virtually all formal and informal CIO gatherings, and addressed conventions, all at the invitation of President Murray. Monsignor Charles Owen Rice, his parish priest and the most prominent leader of the Association of Catholic Trade Unionists (ACTU), recalled to this writer that the CIO president was in 1945 continuing to hold extended private meetings, as he had during and before the war, with top ACTU and Church leaders to check the left influence in CIO affiliates.[20]

Whatever else may have motivated him, Murray had no personal ideological reason for pushing the CIO into the controversial World Federation of Trade Unions. James B. Carey, secretary-treasurer of the CIO, who was a delegate to various WFTU meetings and on occasion appointed head of a CIO delegation by Murray, often explained to colleagues and staffers that the CIO now had prestige and status equal to the AFL. Carey was a vocal man of the right, but dependent on Philip Murray, who had selected him for his position. Carey duly accepted WFTU assignments given him by President Murray. But he felt he had to justify the WFTU connection, and frequently cited status and prestige, not other reasons. In any event, the WFTU move gave the CIO a role on the world stage, a position of high status. Moreover, by appointing two

---

[19]Murray papers, Catholic University of America, passim; observations of the writer. I discuss the Catholic influence on Murray in more detail in Chapter 5.
[20]Interviews, 1977–8, at the Woodrow Wilson International Center for Scholars and the Cosmos Club, and by phone.

well-known centrists, Hillman and Thomas, to manage the CIO's participation in the new world labor body, Murray was not only helping to stake out for the CIO a new status and prestige in the international field but simultaneously awarding two colleagues with prestigious positions. Also, these two CIO vice-presidents not only were well known at home and abroad, but could not be categorized as communist sympathizers; each had a proven anticommunist record in his union. This record would not only insulate the organization from attacks by federal officials but would also facilitate working with Sir Walter Citrine, who had been for years a staunch fighter against the left in the British TUC. Citrine, for his part, was anxious to placate the Soviet trade union leaders, and was known to object to the AFL's efforts abroad as too crude. At the same time, Hillman and Thomas had proven they could work with the left in the CIO and would be acceptable to Moscow and in the left-led unions in other countries. And it would keep "Tommy" and "Sidney" happy and busy. Hillman assumed the position as top U.S. representative of the CIO in the WFTU executive bureau, on a level with Citrine and V. V. Kuznetsov of the Soviet All-Union Central Council of Trade Unions.

Apart from Murray's many-sided international moves in 1945, all under way prior to his attendance at the president's Labor-Management Conference, he was also influenced by political ties he maintained with the left, and with Hillman and Thomas, through the Political Action Committee of the CIO. Sidney Hillman had been welcomed back by Murray after a frustrating tour of duty in the war agencies. He had been denied AFL support when he sought to gain the position of director of the War Manpower Commission, a position Roosevelt gave to Paul McNutt in a move that I suspect grew out of the fact that McNutt was a Democratic Party leader who had no ties or sympathy with any of the rival union centers. Actually, Hillman had had minimal support from the CIO, which he had helped with funds and by assigning organizing cadres from "the Amalgamated," his own rich union. Murray awarded Sidney Hillman the chairmanship of the CIO PAC in 1943 and then in 1945 chose him as the CIO's representative to the World Federation of Trade Unions. Thomas was equally involved with the PAC, though not in an executive capacity, and shared WFTU junkets.

Whether or not Murray acted out of considerations of status or patronage in pushing the World Federation of Trade Unions, he had put the CIO into a new confrontational position with both Lewis and the American Federation of Labor hierarchy on the eve of Truman's Labor-Management Conference, which opened in Washington in November 1945. This new labor split occurred at the very time that the manufacturers under NAM leadership were gearing up for a united postwar plan of attack on the unions' legal and organizational status.

The complexities of Philip Murray's personality are beyond the scope of this study. Yet one should not exclude Phil Murray's antipathy toward John L. Lewis from the factors motivating him. As the Labor-Management Conference would soon reveal, fear and hatred defined their relationship, in contrast to the father-son feelings that had characterized the two men in the years they shared top leadership of the Miners and the CIO.

The President's Labor-Management Conference of 1945

Amidst the rejoicing that followed the unconditional surrender of Japan on August 14, 1945, little notice was taken of quiet plans for the president's moves toward postwar industrial peace. This "peace" plan has usually been taken as a sign of governmental and industrial acceptance of collective bargaining. But the reality is more complex. Even the origination of the idea for a conference is uncertain. What is certain is that labor demonstrated its fragmentation and a predominance of laissez-faire thinking, while business showed solidarity and political determination.

The Truman administration, as we have seen, gave mixed signals on its postwar labor policies. While retaining some New Dealers, Truman was pulling away from New Deal–type collaboration with labor, particularly the CIO. By late 1945, President Truman and his cabinet were giving priority to the forging of a new bipartisan coalition for international policy. As a practical Democratic politician, ex-Senator Truman of course knew that he had to make concrete overtures and concessions to the Republicans, especially those in the Senate. He came up with an ideological handshake – strong unity for atomic diplomacy; against the foreign foe, the Soviet bloc; and against the left at home. This emerging bipartisanship inevitably shaped the administration's domestic labor policy as well as its foreign policy; and it helped to further aggravate AFL/CIO differences and factional differences within the CIO. The American Federation of Labor, bipartisan for generations, had long ago attained ideological conformity on international affairs. In 1945, its political commitments abroad were strong but did not interfere with its traditional anticommunist demonology, either at home or abroad.[21]

[21] Anthony Carew, "The Schism Within the World Federation of Trade Unions: Government and Trade Union Diplomacy," *International Review of Social History,* 24 (1984), pp. 297–335. Carew sees the AFL as pressing the Trades Union Congress to break with the WFTU, and cites Citrine's irritation with the crudely anticommunist, anti-Soviet "style" of the AFL and the

The first meetings of the Labor-Management Conference were called by Secretary of Labor Schwellenbach and the secretary of commerce, Henry A. Wallace. These first meetings seem to have excluded labor entirely. They included the blue-ribbon business groups of corporate executives known as the Business Advisory Council housed at Commerce, and the leaders of the National Association of Manufacturers.[22]

Though not formally invited to the first meetings at this early planning stage, the top leaders of labor seem to have been informally consulted regarding their willingness to participate as well as on their preferences for representation. The labor bodies were officially consulted at all subsequent stages. While the degree of their participation at the first stage of planning remains speculative, we know that the leaders of labor fought about who would represent labor. Conflicting responses to the president and the secretary of labor divided the world of labor, but the conflict had little to do with such class-based interests as shares of income, the legal rights of workers to organize, or the mounting offensive of management designed to reassert its prewar hostility to good-faith bargaining. Instead, and again, each of the labor groups was seeking to present and defend its institutional interests.

There were other splits in labor's ranks besides the basic AFL/CIO rivalry, the CIO factionalism, and the UMW's independence. When Truman's cabinet began planning labor's representation to the president's Labor-Management Conference, it came up against the problem of representation for the railroad unions. The unaffiliated railroad brotherhoods, for many years proudly independent, were officially excluded. Instead, the AFL-affiliated Railway Labor Executives Association's T. G. Cashen – perhaps mistakenly; perhaps because of pressure by Lewis or Green – was chosen by the planners to represent the million or so railroad workers. The Washington representative of the Brotherhood of Railroad Trainmen (BRT), Martin Miller, identified the BRT as the "largest of the independent railroad unions" and in a November 5,

---

rivalry between the TUC and the AFL for "leadership of the international movement." The CIO's belated decision in 1949 to join the AFL in forming a new world labor body, the International Confederation of Free Trade Unions (ICFTU), as an anticommunist center is attributed to the shift in "balance of power" between "pro- and anti-Communists in the CIO." Carew concludes from his study, mainly based on official British Foreign Office and U.S. State Department documents: "The CIO's main pre-occupation was a more narrowly focused rivalry with the AFL for organizational dominance in the United States" (pp. 333–4).

[22]Based on an unsigned and undated memorandum in Secretary Schwellenbach's papers (U.S. Archives, Department of Labor, Secretary's files, box 174, "Labor-Management Conference" folder). The memo was apparently written by a corporate executive named Smith, and it is not clear whether he or she represented the Business Advisory Council or the NAM. The memo states that agreement was reached on agenda procedures and representation but not on location of the conference.

1945, letter to Secretary Schwellenbach insisted that A. F. Whitney, president of the Trainmen, should have been chosen to represent the brotherhoods.

"[It was] a violation of democratic procedure to have Mr. Cashen, who heads an AF of L organization, designated as the spokesman for the independent Railroad Brotherhoods," Mr. Miller wrote. "Under no circumstances will he [Cashen] be permitted to represent the B. of R.T. Furthermore, in order that there may be no misunderstanding, I desire to say that the Brotherhood of Railroad Trainmen will not be influenced or bound by any action taken by the so-called Labor-Management Conference convening today in Washington, D.C. . . . You must know," Miller added, "that Mr. Cashen's union is affiliated with the A.F. of L.; therefore to allow the Railway Labor Executives Association to choose the representative of the independent Railroad Brotherhoods is to deny the Brotherhoods the representation to which they are entitled, while granting the AFL an additional voice in the Conference."[23] BRT president Whitney himself told Schwellenbach "that the Brotherhood of Railroad Trainmen due to the politics in labor, could not consistently authorize Mr. Cashen to represent it at said conference. . . . The BRT," he concluded, "will not participate."[24]

The Vandenberg Connection

An intriguing and unexplored political intersection of domestic and international affairs occurred through Arthur H. Vandenberg, the senior senator from Michigan, best known as the head of the Republican delegation to the United Nations' founding meeting in San Francisco. Although identified by most observers of the period with foreign relations and the burgeoning Cold War, Vandenberg also figured quietly but importantly in the original decision to call the conference. The Michigan senator, regarded by people in his state as the voice of the car manufacturers, had been active against the Wagner Act and the National Labor Relations Board in the late 1930s. In 1940, when he himself was trying for the Republican presidential nomination, he wrote, "Society sees just as much need for protection against union dictators as against employer dictators."[25] During the war, he shifted from isolationism to vigorous support of an activist U.S. foreign policy. He remained a Hamiltonian Republican Party leader. On July 30, 1945, Senator Vandenberg resumed

[23]U.S. Archives, Department of Labor, Secretary's files, box 174, "Labor-Management Conference" folder.
[24]Ibid.
[25]*Nation*, May 11, 1940, "Man Who Would Be President," p. 410.

his interest in labor matters, initiating extensive correspondence about an "Industrial Peace Conference." Tying the idea to changing international developments, he wrote to labor secretary Schwellenbach, suggesting a labor-management meeting for peace "at home."[26] He refrained from an attack on the Wagner Act and accepted the principle of collective bargaining. However, "to keep our industrial machine going," he thought the issue before the conferees should be strikes, which he knew were sanctioned under the Wagner Act. He also implied that other welfare-state measures ("social and economic standards, etc.") should be excluded from labor policy consideration:

It [the proposed "peace conference"] will richly justify itself if it can help to keep our industrial machine going – for the common goal of all concerned and for the public welfare – while this other question "social and economic standards, etc." are settled by other (and perhaps similar) methods.

Vandenberg was more precise about the Wagner Act in concurrent correspondence with the famous anti-union industrialist Ernest T. Weir, to whom he wrote that the essential problem was "to keep our industrial machine going."[27] This implied a curbing of the right to strike, the weapon that he and other Michigan public figures knew had been used by labor in the 1930s to bring auto makers and other Michigan industrialists to bargaining tables.

The urbane Michigander now coupled his idea for a conference with acceptance of collective bargaining while also making clear to his correspondents what he knew from earlier efforts on behalf of Michigan industrialists: Curbing the right to strike could be accomplished only by amending the Wagner Act.

The senator's intervention influenced the labor policies of the administration. Schwellenbach and Truman were also broadly committed to the principles of collective bargaining. Moreover, in the Labor Department, holdover personnel from New Deal days were still pressing the secretary to reaffirm the wisdom and appropriateness of the National Labor Relations Act, a keystone act of the New Deal. This bureaucratic clinging to the Wagner Act is reflected in reporting on the Twelfth National Conference on Labor Legislation, hosted by the department:

"State anti-labor laws" were being enacted to curb strikes, outlawing closed or union shops, peaceful picketing and "other legitimate organization activities"; with apparent approval, the Department cited the Conference decision to condemn "all current at-

---

[26]Michigan Historical Collections, Bentley Historical Library, University of Michigan, letter from Vandenberg to Schwellenbach, July 30, 1945.

[27]Ibid., letter from Vandenberg to Weir, president of the Weirton Steel Company, August 7, 1945.

tempts to emasculate the National Labor Relations Act by partial repeal or amendment . . ."28

President Truman had a record in the Senate of being pro-labor. From my own observations, I knew he had active support from CIO PAC chairman Hillman for the vice-presidency at the 1944 Democratic Party convention. But he too, worried by the growing pattern of unofficial and official stoppages in 1944–5, had become doubtful about continuation of the Wagner Act. In his memoirs, he wrote of this period of labor-law debate: "The Wagner Labor Relations Act [*sic*] of 1935 . . . was a great step forward, even though experience showed it needed amendment – but I wanted it properly amended."29

There was more to this than labor law. The spirit of the New Deal was involved. When R. J. Thomas, UAW-CIO president and CIO vice-president and chairman of its Housing Committee, wrote Truman about what Thomas felt was an impending housing shortage, asking support for legislation to increase the supply of moderate-income housing, and asked, "Are we willing to admit that we can't solve such problems in the present time, without the military urgency?" Truman reacted by referring to some of the unauthorized auto strikes. In ordering a reply, he attached a handwritten note to his assistant, Judge Samuel Rosenman. He ignored the housing question altogether on this buckslip note; instead, the president expressed his extreme irritation about the first postwar strikes then under way in the automobile industry: "Tell him [Thomas] that if he'll get his gang back to work, the things referred to here can be worked out."30

The role of Senator Vandenberg was not discussed within the CIO. It is unlikely that Lewis and the AFL were aware of his role or cared what it was. An old foe of the Wagner Act since New Deal days, Vandenberg had worked with AFL attorneys in the late 1930s to restrict and amend the act. As indicated above, Vandenberg was persuaded that this "peace" conference could at least result in a restoration of management authority by curbing strikes, and at best result in changing the Wagner Act.31

28U.S. Department of Labor, *Twelfth National Conference on Labor Legislation: Résumé of Proceedings*, Bulletin No. 76 (Washington, D.C.: Government Printing Office, 1946), pp. 27–8. The National Conference on Labor Legislation was held during the president's Labor-Management Conference, on December 5 and 6, 1945.

29Harry S. Truman, *Memoirs* (New York: Doubleday, 1955), pp. 149–50.

30The note to Judge Rosenman and the letter from Thomas to Truman are quoted in Joseph Goulden, *The Best Years: 1945–1960* (New York: Atheneum, 1976), p. 120.

31Vandenberg's hope for a broad amendment to the NLRA is expressed in the August 7, 1945, letter to Weir, an old foe of the Wagner Act. Weir was skeptical that the conference would yield the desired result, but Vandenberg indicated that he thought the meeting would be an important step in that direction.

The president of the United States, already doubtful about Wagner and now developing a friendship with his former Senate colleague based on their common interests in the emerging activist foreign policy, wanted higher industrial production, not strike interruptions. (We come back to the politics of labor law when discussing Truman's veto of Taft-Hartley in Chapter 4.) On the event, the Truman administration grabbed at Senator Vandenberg's "peace" proposal. Somewhat ambiguously, the administration went to some lengths to credit him with the idea of a postwar meeting while itself claiming to have considered such a meeting "for some time." Referring to the senator's letter of July 30, 1945, Secretary Schwellenbach in his official report quoted that part of the Vandenberg letter urging that a meeting be held to "lay the groundwork for peace and justice on the home front":

The problem of how to deal with labor-management difficulties in the postwar period had been under discussion between President Truman and the Secretary of Labor for some time [wrote Schwellenbach, and] the message from Senator *Vandenberg served to crystallize the decision to go ahead with the conference at the earliest possible moment.*[32]

President Truman in his conference-opening remarks on November 5, 1945, said nothing about the Vandenberg role and left the impression that the delegates themselves would decide postwar policy: "Each of you is now a member of the team which will recommend definite labor policy in the field of industrial relations."[33]

As Vandenberg had done in his letter to Schwellenbach, however, Truman emphasized the need for uninterrupted production to meet American postwar responsibilities. He referred to strikes obliquely. Borrowing language proposed by Vandenberg, he said that "subversive attacks upon essential production are the gravest threats to the permanent success of Labor's Bill of Rights [Vandenberg's term for the Wagner Act]."[34] Whatever the source of his language, the president was making clear that stoppages of production were perceived by him as a threat to his domestic and international policies. The labor delegates and institutions were divided on both questions. John L. Lewis was the only labor leader to publicly link domestic and foreign policies; he did so from the right. He also noted the absence of labor unity while proclaiming

[32]U.S. Department of Labor, "Labor-Management Conference on Industrial Relations," *Monthly Labor Review,* January 1946, p. 37; U.S. Archives, Department of Labor, Secretary's files, box 174, "Labor-Management Conference" folder (emphasis supplied).
[33]Ibid.
[34]U.S. Archives, Department of Labor, Secretary's files, box 174, "Labor-Management Conference" folder, "Verbatim Plenary Session," November 5, 1945.

the resistance of labor "to any foreign foe." He told the press after the president's conference ended: "One great lesson to American labor from this Conference is the fact that it has been demonstrated that labor has a job to do in America on its own household, in the unification of its own policies and the bringing close together its own leadership." Lewis said he believed that "any foreign foe or those who would destroy us would not be able to undermine our American institutions."[35] The latter point may have been a veiled attack on the CIO and Murray for CIO international moves, or a reference to the Mine Workers' determination, expressed forcefully by Lewis at the conference, to proceed with its own brand of business unionism.

At the president's conference, all the labor delegates demonstrated their readiness to defend traditional collective bargaining. They publicly squabbled, however, not only over representation but on how the bargaining system should work. Their squabbles on the latter point bordered on the ridiculous.

For its approach to the president's Labor-Management Conference, the CIO's own internal conflicts were swept under the rug. As noted, the executive board in November of 1945 unanimously endorsed participation. It is interesting to note, in view of subsequent congressional and scholarly debate over the issue of political influence in CIO-led postwar strikes (see Chapter 3), that Murray saw these strikes as employer-instigated. He told the 1946 UAW-CIO convention that he had tried to gain support from other labor leaders at the conference for a general wage increase in the hope of setting a government-approved postwar wage pattern without the "calamity" of strikes.[36]

Conflict and Farce at the Labor Tables

John L. Lewis was probably the unnamed target of Murray's "calamity" comment. Although Lewis pointed to the necessity of unity among labor unions when assessing the results of the Labor-Management Conference, Lewis himself underscored the deepening rift among union leaders when he directly attacked Philip Murray during a floor discussion on the subject of postwar wage policy. Speaking for the CIO delegation, Murray had tried to project CIO wage policy on the floor of the conference. He had first attempted, prior to the meeting, to gain support for the proposition that industrial peace required that a general wage increase be granted by employers.

[35]*New York Times*, November 30, 1945.
[36]UAW-CIO Convention, Atlantic City, N.J., 1946, *Proceedings*, p. 152.

Lewis and Green objected, each arguing that the market should determine wage settlements. Murray's motion therefore failed, the labor group having adopted a unanimity rule before the conference began.

Having lost his move within the labor group, Murray introduced the question of a wage increase on the floor of the meeting itself. When he did, however, Lewis took the floor and charged that the CIO unions in auto and steel were "afraid" to face their employers and were trying to get the Truman administration to work out a formula to help them settle the negotiations then pending. The preposterous Lewis-Murray "dialogue" (as reported on the front page of the *New York Times*) follows:

Murray: "The CIO is not afraid of anybody and I am not afraid of you."
"Nuts," Mr. Lewis said.
"Nuts to you," replied Mr. Murray.[37]

Insofar as this exchange reflected the antagonism between Lewis and Murray, and their changing relationship, one may view the incident as trivial. But one cannot overlook the fact that the two most prominent labor leaders of the era were not merely individuals, but representatives at this seminal conference of the U.S. labor movement. While many who knew and watched Murray and Lewis tended to dismiss the dialogue as another example of the love-hate relationship that characterized "John" and "Phil," the exchange of juvenile insults dramatized the tragic split of labor during the most publicized labor-policy debates since enactment of the Wagner Act in 1935.

The John L. Lewis Factor

Murray may have been the immediate butt of Lewis' barbs. But the entire CIO now viewed Lewis as an enemy largely because of his distancing himself from first Roosevelt and now Truman and the national Democratic Party. He was already engaged in bargaining for the Mine Workers–managed health and welfare system he negotiated in 1946. For the CIO in 1945 – left and right and center – preservation of New Deal labor legislation was the one political issue they all agreed upon. The railroad brotherhoods, thanks to the Railway Labor Act of 1926, were also highly government-dependent, through a national mediation board, for their bargaining system (but were not beholden to the Democratic Party). The AFL leaders, as well as Lewis, while adhering in 1944 and 1945 to political neutrality, were concentrating on market-based

[37]*New York Times,* November 9, 1945. Louis Stark, the *Times'* internationally known senior labor correspondent, covered all the sessions.

collective bargaining. Lewis, one should recall, prior to his breakaway had for many years sat on the AFL executive council, where he was not known to differ with the prevailing view of the labor barons who all favored Gompers' political neutralism. During his brief CIO presidency, he frequently charged that such a philosophy, appropriate for a laissez-faire period, was obsolete in the evolving mixed economy. Accordingly, Lewis had made the CIO a part of the New Deal coalition by 1936. Now that he was out of the CIO, he was back to laissez-faire.

The changing role of the state could hardly be defined with accuracy by any of the actors present at the 1945 conference, but the CIO at least recognized that the state was going to be vital for labor. The rest of labor did not see as yet that the government's new role demanded a labor position. As Selig Perlman had prophesied, the CIO created a political machinery in 1943 for its survival and growth. This move placed it in conflict not only with conservatives but also with the rest of labor. There can be little doubt that factional, prestige, and patronage factors influenced the CIO to create the PAC. However, in addition and more basically, the CIO's political differences with the AFL, and with the Miners, were based on the perception of CIO leaders that their unions had not yet fully consolidated their objectives; in order to do so, the CIO simply needed continued government protection and assistance. As for John L. Lewis, he was confident of preserving the UMWA and gaining new victories for his members in the postwar era through collective bargaining. The Miners would not go along with the notion that labor solidarity and labor political action were necessary; the UMWA would go it alone if necessary, as that union had done in the past. Yet the UMWA and Lewis were probably also determined to catch up with the manufacturing unions, whose workers had surpassed the coal miners in hourly earnings.[38] Lewis' imminent and brief return to the American Federation of Labor (see Chapter 5) may have been an additional factor in his public espousal of a laissez-faire philosophy.

In going beyond an expression of scorn for CIO president Murray, Lewis underscored his own reversion to laissez-faire. With characteristic drama, he expressed the broad philosophy of the Miners, coupling his reversion to market unionism with an attack on the CIO "formula" and opposing with scorn "all its manifestations":

The miners could not afford to vote for a resolution offered by the CIO that bound labor at a cost of living formula, giving labor a chance to advance its wages only as the price

[38]Harold G. Vatter, *The Mixed Economy in World War II* (New York: Columbia University Press, 1986).

of milk, children's shoes or straw hats advances. . . . We say we are for free enterprise. We are opposed to the corporate state and all its manifestations as expressed in the CIO resolution. . . . The rest of us don't need to throw up our hands in despair because two great corporations are not getting along with their labor organizations. . . . there is no pessimism about the future in the stock market or bonds. They are both rising. America is sound. As President Garfield said, "God reigns and the flag still flies over the Capitol in Washington."[39]

In his unvarnished, hyperbolic defense of free enterprise and the market, Lewis was not only expressing his contempt for his former aid Murray but setting himself apart from the mass unions. While Lewis' speech may be seen as voicing confidence in labor's bargaining power, it may also be viewed as a contributing factor to labor's political paralysis and hence as a symbol of labor's vulnerability.

Lewis might also have had some tongue in his ample cheek. The UMWA continued to press government on miner-related issues. During his presidency, the UMWA had done so prior to, during, and after its CIO connection. Or, equally plausible, Lewis could have been guided by the strong competitive view he held about the CIO in union matters. In any event, the entire management team at the president's conference expressed glowing pleasure at Lewis' speech. Their delegation agreed that the speech in which Lewis distanced himself from Murray was "one of the best speeches on free enterprise that they had ever heard."[40]

As for the employer side, by the time of the president's conference the differences between Johnston and the NAM reflected in the spring charter signing had vanished. "Solidarity Forever" could have been the theme song of the combined Chamber-NAM team in November-December. When signing the Management-Labor Charter early in 1945, Johnston seemed to accept the

[39]*New York Times*, November 9, 1945. John Brophy, a well-known figure from the UMWA, who was for years closely associated in the UMWA and the CIO with Lewis, attributes to Lewis some of the basic characteristics the Webbs found in their evaluation of British craft union leaders. Lewis, Brophy wrote to Walter Reuther in 1954, was "the exponent of a curious form of laisse fair [*sic*]"; he "inconsistently urges all forms of government assistance for his industry." But he accepted "business domination of the economy" and had a basic distrust of the "common man" and a "nineteenth century outlook" (Walter P. Reuther collection, Series II, box 3, Brophy memorandum to Reuther [then CIO president], May 5, 1954, "Some comments on recent Lewis address").

The UMSA quit the CIO in 1940 over Lewis' differences with Roosevelt. In 1946, Lewis reaffiliated the Miners with the AFL, staying as an affiliate until 1947, when he sent his imperious note to William Green: "Green, we disaffiliate." This action followed Lewis' defeat over signing the Taft-Hartley "anticommunist" or "loyalty" affidavits, discussed in Chapter 5. For evaluation of Lewis as a leader, including some of his dealings with President Roosevelt, see James McGregor Burns, *Leadership* (New York: Harper & Row, 1978), pp. 435–6.

[40]*New York Times*, November 9, 1945.

federal labor-relations law and the transfer of some power at the workplace. Now, only six months later, Johnston joined the NAM-led team demanding a reassertion of traditional management authority – an issue that became the key to success or failure of the elaborately planned conference.

Management at the president's conference argued for a general rollback of union power at the workplace and at the negotiating tables. Though neither collective bargaining per se, the Wagner Act, nor the political beliefs of labor leaders were challenged at the conference, the arguments advanced for restoration of management rights amounted to a demand for change in labor law and, if the unions refused, voluntary acceptance of pre-union relationships between capital and labor. The offensive taken by management delegates was perhaps spurred by Walter Reuther's unprecedented challenge to heretofore sacred management territory: his demand for a look at the books of General Motors to determine whether the corporation could afford to pay a substantial wage increase without any rise in prices. In addition, the management team members were alarmed by the National Labor Relations Board ruling that foremen, though salaried, were workers and should therefore be permitted to vote under the Wagner Act for or against a union. That ruling was taken as a threat to all manufacturers. The industry delegates asked for voluntary agreement by both sides that a curb should be imposed on the NLRB against such an interpretation of the law.

In a united response, labor delegates finessed the question. Stating that they agreed in principle that the "functions and responsibilities of management must be preserved if business and industry is to be efficient, progressive, and provide more good jobs," the union officials went on to declare that they refused to "build a fence around the rights and responsibilities of management on one hand and the unions on the other."[41]

In this unusual demonstration of unity, labor avoided the divisive questions of the preservation of the basic labor statute and government intervention in general. Those remained as points of dispute within labor. The joint labor objection seemed to be based on the leaders' feelings that union fundamentals – seniority, production standards, and other traditional contractual agreements obtained by collective bargaining – would be placed in jeopardy. This was not a sign of political agreement.

Only the CIO delegates – all deeply committed to partisan politics – were voicing concern that management would respond by going to Congress. Other labor delegates clung to a traditional market-based laissez-faire philosophy.

[41]U.S. Department of Labor, *Report,* op. cit., p. 51.

They apparently assumed that industry would do so as well. However, the management group now drew their own political conclusions:

Since . . . labor members . . . have been unwilling to agree on any listing of specific management functions [we] conclude that the labor members are convinced that the field of collective bargaining will, in all probability, continue to expand into the management field. The only possible end of such a philosophy would be joint management of the enterprise.[42]

The odd and ironic twist in these positions was that most of labor – the Miners and the AFL – wanted to stick to the market. Management would forgo laissez-faire and go to Congress.

For management delegates, the legal classification of foremen was intimately linked with the general problem of management rights. Mounting a campaign against the Wagner Act – a law that enabled the CIO to help organize foremen and other supervisory people in industrial plants – was therefore a logical political step. The corporate response was: "[If executives] cannot properly . . . function without assistance [it follows] that there be no unionization of any part of management." Also, since foremen were supervisors and exercised managerial authority, any organization into unions for purposes of collective bargaining "would mean that unions had taken over both sides of the bargaining table." Again, the labor delegation finessed the proposed exemption of supervisory employees, replying that "it would be inappropriate to make any recommendation on the matter of unionization of foremen while cases involving this issue are pending before the National Labor Relations Board."[43]

The Taft-Hartley Act of 1947 specifically barred foremen from the protection of the revised labor law and the reconstructed NLRB. That exclusion led to the demise of the Foremen's Association of America, which was probably a significant factor in the U.S. postwar decline of labor. There was by 1945 already in process a vast increase in the number of nonproduction supervisory and administrative people in the labor force. This process has continued to change the profile of the workforce and the structure of unionism in all industrialized countries. In Britain, for example, employees classified as "foremen and related supervisory occupations" had been organizing in basic industry since World War I, and during the post–World War II era had become one of the fastest-growing Trades Union Congress affiliates.[44] In the United States in 1945, the CIO was anticipating affiliation of the then unaffiliated

[42]Ibid., p. 53.   [43]Ibid., pp. 51–3.
[44]Irving Richter, *Political Purpose in Trade Unions* (London: Allen & Unwin, 1973), pp. 132ff.

Foremen's Association of America as a consequence of the NLRB determination on March 25, 1945 (later upheld by the U.S. Supreme Court) that "general foremen, assistant foremen and special assignment persons [employed at the Detroit plants of Packard Motor Car Company] constitute a unit appropriate for the purpose of collective bargaining."[45] When the NLRB ruled in favor of organizing foremen and related occupations in 1945, it provided an added incentive to management to unite politically and achieve this ban, along with other legislative restrictions on labor organizations, by congressional action. The strikes of 1945–6 unwittingly helped bring about the Wagner Act revisions, long sought by the act's opponents in industry. These strikes, their economic and political causes, and their political results are examined next.

[45]Murray papers, Catholic University of America, box 23.

3

THE GREAT STRIKE WAVE OF 1946
AND ITS POLITICAL
CONSEQUENCES

When the Second World War ended, only a small minority of the general public favored a law barring strikes in peacetime.[1] Yet the majority of the voting public put into office a Republican Congress in the elections of 1946, which acted on the belief that the giant postwar strike wave was politically inspired, the product of "communist" and "subversive" influences. The 80th Congress in 1947 enacted what labor unions universally termed the "Slave-Labor" law. The Labor-Management Relations (Taft-Hartley) Act – passed over President Truman's veto – inaugurated drastic changes in the New Deal labor law, the National Labor Relations (Wagner) Act. While the new labor law continued the governmental policy favoring collective bargaining, it was atavistic. Among many other changes, Taft-Hartley barred supervisors from Labor Board protection; restricted the right of unions with respect to striking; and, acting on the belief that it was communists and fellow travelers who were responsible for the great postwar strike wave, imposed in Section 9(h) a loyalty test on union officers. Under Section 9(h), unions wishing to use the reconstructed Labor Board's services would be required to have their officers each year sign what the union leadership generally termed a "loyalty" or "noncommunist" affidavit. Enforcement of that particular provision by the reconstructed National Labor Relations Board and the Department of Justice, as well as the unions' own ambivalence, resulted in further division of an already highly fragmented labor movement. The latter point, developed in detail in Chapter 5, is worth emphasizing here.

Despite passionate union rhetoric about the "slave-labor" law, most unions rushed to sign the affidavits. At the CIO, several unions developed political action to halt enforcement and, later, to amend or repeal the new act. But the

---

[1] Rita James Simon, *Public Opinion in America, 1936–1970* (Chicago: Rand McNally, 1974), p. 17. The polls conducted by the American Institute of Public Opinion showed the percentage favoring barring of strikes at 24 in 1944 and 28 in 1947.

most serious debate, at the CIO and inside the AFL, was over compliance with the "noncommunist" Section 9(h). In many cases, the subject of signing and complying – and even how far beyond the law itself one should go to assure eligibility under the statute's requirement – became the central concern. Section 9(h) grew out of a rich mix of political soil and climate. This provision – and the numerous other restrictions in Taft-Hartley – was justified in the view of congressional figures, Democrats as well as Republicans, by evidence showing "political" influence in striking unions, notably in Local 248, UAW-CIO, at the West Allis (Wisconsin) plant of the Allis-Chalmers Company. This stoppage, still in progress when the new labor bill was being debated in the spring of 1947, became a vehicle for a wide-ranging inquiry by Congress into communism in France, Italy, the United States, and the Soviet Union and in West Allis, the home of Local 248. The "communistic" strike at West Allis, as led by Local 248, received inordinate congressional attention. It will be seen as having enormous weight in the legislative debate – far more than has been recognized by observers. This stoppage was of course part of a broader wave of labor actions, but no doubt reinforced the prevailing fears about labor power. How else can one account for the fact that members of Congress generally chose to ignore the most authoritative analysis of the 1946 strike wave and its underlying causes, issued some months before the hearings by the Bureau of Labor Statistics (BLS) of the United States Department of Labor, "Postwar Work Stoppages Caused by Labor-Management Disputes"? The BLS reported 4,750 stoppages in 1945. The Local 248 walkout was but one of 4,985 called in 1946. By 1946, a total of 4.6 million workers were directly involved in stoppages, a figure larger than in any previous year on record. Measured by total time lost, there were 116 million man-days of idleness resulting from stoppages, or 1.45 percent of total working time. By comparison, the total strike idleness at the height of the CIO's sitdown strikes in 1936–7 was only 0.5 percent of total working time, one-third that of 1946.[2]

Like other great events associated with World War II and its aftermath, the great 1946 strike specter can be treated as a political phenomenon. But the Bureau of Labor Statistics summary report published immediately after the record-breaking strike wave was over calmly pointed to economic causation:

Wages were a major issue in most controversies. Protection of workers' "take-home" pay was emphasized in many of the earlier reconversion wage disputes, but later [in 1946] after the easing and subsequent abandonment of price controls, demands for pay increases to match rising living costs became more frequent.[3]

[2] U.S. Department of Labor, "Postwar Work Stoppages Caused by Labor-Management Disputes," *Monthly Labor Review,* December 1946, pp. 872–92.
[3] Ibid., pp. 780–1.

The Bureau of Labor Statistics saw the relatively big strikes (including Allis-Chalmers) as well as the smaller ones as one part of economic readjustment, and an indication merely of differences between the two sides over postwar bargaining relations:

Workers were concerned about losses in earnings and rises in prices and employers about government controls, reconversion problems, and new markets for their products.[4]

Of course, unions are political as well as economic institutions; political factors therefore enter into many policy decisions. In most unions, a decision whether or not to call a strike becomes a major policy matter. Accordingly, in most unions, whether headed by Democratic, Republican, Socialist, or Communist officers, internal political considerations usually enter into such decisions as whether to announce a strike vote; whether to actually withhold labor collectively; how to finance and otherwise conduct the stoppage (if work is actually brought to a halt); and finally, whether and when to terminate the affair.

In addition to their own internal politics, unions are generally aware – some more than others – of external political imperatives such as governmental policies regarding labor matters in general and strikes in particular. We should recall that unions and stoppages were subjects of congressional investigation many years before Congress enacted any labor law. A Coolidge-era Congress helped politicize labor relations by passage of the Railway Labor Act of 1926, which brought the federal government into that huge and vital sector's labor policies, establishing dispute procedures and granting railroad labor's right to collective bargaining and the right to strike.

With the National Industrial Recovery Act of 1932, often viewed as the beginning of the mixed economy, the government entered into labor as part of a far more massive intervention in the whole economy. This interventionist process led directly to the National Labor Relations Act of 1935, which broadened the rights to bargain and strike. Government intervention in disputes was of course greatly expanded during the defense and wartime years, 1940–5, and continued thereafter. Through all this legislation, the right to strike was recognized as a part of the bargaining process.

Thus, when President Truman called together the Labor-Management Conference shortly after the war ended to consider postwar policy on labor matters, he was pursuing a long-established process of federal intervention. He gave the customary homage to free collective bargaining. The irony escaped

[4]Ibid.

him, but at the same time as he was paying lip service to "free" bargaining, Truman made clear not only by his calling of the conference but also by subsequent actions that the federal government would continue to intrude into and limit the scope of bargaining, particularly in respect to strike action. Writing to CIO president Philip Murray in November of 1945, the president hinted at much broader intervention. The economy of the United States, Truman wrote Murray, "demanded a social contract between labor and management . . . because labor agreements touch not only the lives of wage earners and profits of employers [but] together they affect the stability and balance of the whole economy."[5]

The Truman administration was highly ambivalent. Though invoking the language of social control, it was not proposing either an incomes policy or greater equity in income levels. The president seemed to be nudging recalcitrant management officials to accommodate their labor policies to acceptance of traditional market-based collective bargaining. The major management associations were still refusing to accept the idea of collective bargaining officially and publicly. While divided on the question of bargaining, all were gravitating toward a ban on strikes and other restrictions.

Despite a sharp rise in strike participation, labor set no political demands. The unions were not concerned about income distribution or redistribution. The strike wave cresting in 1946 was largely defensive, as the BLS study quoted above suggested. The strike wave consisted mainly of local unions seeking to maintain for their members bargaining rights and the level of purchasing power achieved during the war. This was the case at Local 248. An additional factor in that strike, overlooked by the authors of Taft-Hartley and members of the Committees on Education and Labor, was the union's insistence on maintaining the union security clause won during the war under War Labor Board auspices. While rigidly adhering to the wartime no-strike pledge, this union, like many others, had made significant inroads against what management preferred to see as its prerogatives. The company, however, was determined to roll back union security and union power at the workplace. In the words of an authority on Allis-Chalmers Company history, "Essentially, Allis-Chalmers negotiators wanted to return to the preunion era of the 1930's."[6]

---

[5]Letter to Philip Murray, president of the CIO, November 8, 1945, reproduced from the collections of the Archives of Labor History and Urban Affairs, Wayne State University, Detroit, CIO file.

[6]Stephen Meyer, "The State and the Workplace: New Deal Labor Policy, the UAW, and Allis-Chalmers in the 1930s and 1940s" (unpublished paper, Lake Forest College, 1984). In "Technology and the Workplace" (unpublished paper, 1984), Meyer focuses on the earlier technological development and labor policies at West Allis.

Strikes are rarely popular. Yet in the United States, as in other industrial societies, the workers' right to strike has been an important part of the evolution of democracy itself. Without the right to threaten strikes and to actually cease work collectively when deemed necessary, working people and their organizations would have no weapon comparable to the employers' lockout weapon. Without the strike weapon, bargaining might proceed. But history tells us that the terms reached under such conditions would likely be against the interests of employees, being based on unilateral decision making by the employer.

In the mid 1940s, however, the country still retained fresh memories of CIO-led organizing strikes in the mass-production industries in the mid 1930s. A few years earlier the coal miners, after years of bitter and often losing strike struggles, had re-formed their own national union. Under John L. Lewis, the United Mine Workers helped finance, and often provided leadership to, workers seeking unions in mass-production industries. Lewis was revered in the auto plants for his strike leadership and his organizing help. Homer Martin, the ex-minister who was the first international president of the United Auto Workers, gave recognition to Lewis but gave even more dramatic expression to the value of the strike weapon as utilized by pioneer rank and filers in the auto industry in 1935–7. After giving due respect to John L. Lewis and his Miners associates for their organizing skills, Martin aroused a 1937 convention of auto workers by reminding them that their strikes were the real source of Lewis' power, forcing open-shop employers to sign their first contracts. It was not Lewis' charisma nor the UMWA funds but the sitdown strike of 1936–7 by General Motors workers in the plants at Flint that forced GM to the bargaining table. After recounting the spontaneous closing of operations by the sitdowners at Fisher No. 1 and Fisher No. 2 plants, Martin recited and won applause for a litany of successive strike victories and the contracts won by similar organizing strikes:

(1) A contract was won at Briggs Manufacturing in Detroit, by Local 212, UAW, "in the very heart of open shop reaction."
(2) "We will not forget that the Hudson workers also signed an agreement with their corporation after a great strike."
(3) "We will not forget that the Packard workers also signed an agreement with their great corporation after a great strike." The list went on.[7]

By 1946, in the cities of Flint, Detroit, Pittsburgh, and Milwaukee and other great industrial centers, and on the docks and ships and in the terminals

[7]UAW-CIO Convention, 1937, *Proceedings*, pp. 218–19.

of San Francisco, New York, and other ports, collective bargaining contracts were in place. Most had been preceded by recognition strikes.

In the immediate postwar era when the Democratic administration was ambivalent about labor policy, it was difficult for the public to get a balanced picture of the role of strikes or stoppages in the system of labor relations. As the great journalist Walter Lippmann has noted somewhere in his vast writings, serious attention to the labor question is rare in the typical daily newspaper. Labor reporters, Lippmann wrote, tend to make mountains out of molehills and molehills out of mountains. This could equally be said of the 1946 crop of influential but generally anti-union columnists and radio news commentators.

Strikes and Bargaining

A useful perspective on the nonpolitical aspects of the postwar strike wave in the United States may be facilitated by a British study made shortly after a more recent rash of strikes in that country's motor-car industry. Here too it was widely believed in Whitehall, Parliament, and the media that the Communist Party was unduly influential in the calling and conduct of the stoppages. In 1964, a group of Cambridge University specialists in industrial relations decided to undertake an unusual and extended participant-observer study of what the media termed "unofficial" strikes. After close study of behavior in the plants and extended interviews with strikers and management, they reached conclusions that should illuminate the roles played by politics and publicity in any general movement for stopping work:

Like all conflicts, strikes attract an audience, which sees them from different angles. . . . There seems currently, for instance, an almost universal assumption that strikes are bad, that they are necessarily manifestations of darkness rather than light in the process of industrial adaptation and change. While opposed, [another] but very much minority opinion holds practically all strikes justifiable.[8]

By mid 1946, there was a rising clamor in the USA, including some cries from labor, against "political" strikes. The president and the Democratic House seemed convinced that subversion was a significant force propelling workers into stoppages. The leading Senate Republicans, Taft and Vandenberg, agreed. This was not, however, the view of the American experts Truman had appointed in 1945 when he first tried to come to terms with postwar stoppages. Professor George W. Taylor (after returning to the Whar-

[8]H. A. Turner, Garfield Clack, and Geoffrey Roberts, *Labour Relations in the Motor Industry* (London: Allen & Unwin, 1967), ch. 7.

ton School at the University of Pennsylvania following his stint in Washington first as a public member of the War Labor Board and then as secretary and manager of the president's 1945 Labor-Management Conference) told a predominantly business audience that strikes furnished "the motive power for agreement" in negotiations between the parties engaged in collective bargaining.[9] In sum, whatever else the system provided and whatever its limitations, the principle of collective bargaining is inextricably bound up with the right to strike.

Strikes and Organized Employers

The National Association of Manufacturers, it will be recalled, had been empowered by business leaders specifically to resist all New Deal–sponsored protections of collective bargaining. The point here is that antipathy to unions and to the New Deal labor policy, not "communism" or "socialism," was the main historic impulse behind NAM-led opposition. Those political slogans, and fears, were no doubt present in some industrialists' minds, as indeed they were in many workers'. But the real fear of organized business – whatever the sloganizing – was worker power and unionism.

The NAM had long recognized that strikes by employees had been both a symbol and a practical means of converting individual resentments and desires into collective action. As long ago as its 12th Annual Convention, before the New Deal era and before there was a Communist Party in the United States, the NAM had declared that in its view "industrial peace" could not be achieved if labor collectively used strike weaponry:

Mutually satisfactory wages and working conditions could only be worked out *individually* between employer and employee, and at no time should the employer be intimidated by *threat of strikes,* nor should he be required to resort to the lockout. These principles are matters not of capital against labor, nor employers against employees, but . . . of good citizenship against bad citizenship . . . of Americanism and *patriotism* against demagogism and socialism.[10]

Ten years before the 1946 strike wave, at the height of the CIO drive, the NAM warned its member firms about recognition strikes and instructed them on how to break such strikes. In the *Labor Relations Bulletin* for July 20,

[9]George W. Taylor and A. M. Paxson, "A Pattern for Industrial Peace," in *Proceedings of a Conference Sponsored Jointly by the Economic and Business Foundation and the Mahoning Valley (Pennsylvania) Foremen's Association,* May 16, 1946.

[10]National Association of Manufacturers, *Proceedings of the 12th Annual Convention,* Committee on Resolutions reporting on "Industrial Peace," as summarized and quoted in Robert A. Brady, *Business as a System of Power* (New York: Columbia University Press, 1943), p. 278 (emphasis added). See Chapter 1, n. 4, for the NAM's declaration of policy in 1962.

1936, the NAM urged employers faced with strikes that had been called in order to enforce recognition to employ strike-breaking agencies, send "missionaries" to strikers' homes, and use "armed guards" to turn civil authorities and business and other interests against the striking union through intensive publicity and propaganda. In reporting on the foregoing advice, all part of what came to be known as the Mohawk Valley Formula, the Senate La Follette Committee noted that "deliberate falsehoods and exaggerations" were part of the formula promoted for industry by the NAM.[11]

The senators sponsoring these reports on labor relations prior to the opening of World War II noted a point commonly accepted in the 1930s about industry's labor-relations objectives: to maximize employer power while preventing employees from using their own collective strength at the workplace. Faced in these early efforts with a mounting tide of largely successful organizing strikes, the employer side naturally used divide-and-conquer techniques; they frequently appropriated such terms as "Americanism," "patriotism," and "good citizenship" – all exposed by La Follette Committee investigators as camouflaging resistance to collective bargaining.

We now know that the workers who overcame their differences of creed, race, and gender to achieve organization saw through the employer slogans. Under a relatively unified leadership and with government blessing for collective bargaining, they waved their own American flags, asserting that Americanism, patriotism, and good citizenship did not preclude collective action.[12] When such recalcitrants as General Electric, General Motors, and U.S. Steel, as well as lesser firms such as Allis-Chalmers, were forced to sign contracts, the era of the open shop in American industry had come to an end.

During World War II, as in World War I, NAM member firms and others were forced by the special circumstances of a war economy to bend their principles: first, because the government, which took over control of the economy, had decided it could not effectively prosecute a major war without labor cooperation; second, because market conditions, specifically full employment, favored union growth and union power. All through the war and at

---

[11]U.S. Congress, Senate, Committee on Education and Labor, *Violations of Free Speech and Rights of Labor* (pursuant to S. Res. 266, 74th Cong.), 76th Cong., 1st sess., August 14, 1939, Report No. 6, Part 6, *Labor Policies of Employers' Associations*, Part III: *The National Association of Manufacturers*.

[12]Standard rhetoric of CIO organizers included references to President Roosevelt "wanting" workers to join unions – an exaggeration if not a distortion of that president's real views. Yet there was an understanding among workers in general that the Wagner Act legitimized their collective bargaining goals, even in instances where the pickets were confronted by hostile city and state police forces.

war's end, the New Deal Wagner Act remained intact. In addition, the temporary tripartite National War Labor Board (NWLB) had nudged managers in basic industry and other employers into acceptance of union security protections.

Even Allis-Chalmers, long an opponent of both AFL-affiliated and CIO-affiliated unions and still one of the toughest of NAM members, had found it expedient to go along with a War Labor Board directive to sign a "maintenance of membership" agreement with its CIO-affiliated union, Local 248 of the United Auto Workers. But when the war ended, there was a revival among many NAM-organized firms of traditional resistance to all collective bargaining. As an activist NAM member firm in Milwaukee, the Allis-Chalmers Company became a vital congressional ally for the political attack on the Wagner Act through exploitation of the Local 248 strike and, once again, the popular issue of Americanism.

For many people the mere notion of unions was regarded by 1946 as enough evidence of unpatriotic thinking; the calling of strikes by unions was widely viewed as communism in action. Both the conservative AFL and the new, more militant CIO unions were conducting thousands of walkouts to press their demands. But the CIO unions were attracting more attention, first because they involved more workers, and second because employers and the media could point in many instances to elected radical leaders in the striking locals. And the changing political climate was influencing the top leadership of the CIO as well as its liberal allies. Industry, generally highly organized itself, had never really fully accepted the brash new CIO-type unions that dared to challenge the power of management over its hands. Having failed to win voluntary concessions from labor at the 1945 Labor-Management Conference, many industrialists in 1946 had a new wild card to play: the newly revived Red issue. Original? No! Effective? Decidedly yes!

Favoring the change in political climate, as corporate executives were quite aware, was the tendency among leaders in the CIO itself, as well as in the UAW, the largest CIO affiliate, to move to the right. Philip Murray, who held the reins at the national CIO tight in his hands, having succeeded John L. Lewis as president, was now himself being torn by postwar realignments at home and abroad. On the one hand, Murray, while maintaining his outside affiliations, was forced into a position of leading strikes by CIO unions, whatever their political leadership. He was also still concerned about maintaining the legislative status quo. In that goal, all factions concurred. Addressing the CIO executive board in November 1945, President Murray attributed to management "a real sitdown strike" and lamented the unwillingness of corporate executives to voluntarily settle differences with the new mass unions without the necessity of strikes. He cited the

unwillingness of the employers of the United States to engage themselves in good faith collective bargaining. The employers, as all unions know, I am quite sure, are engaged in a real sitdown strike. . . . There is no evidence or even any wholesome desire on the part of American employers to discuss the respective merits of the Unions of both labor and management or industry.[13]

Murray's statement to the CIO executive board was issued after the CIO failed to gain approval of its voluntarist charter and in apparent anticipation of failure by the 1945 Labor-Management Conference to reach agreement on postwar labor policy. His lament followed on the heels of a joint declaration by the NAM and the Chamber of Commerce of the United States regarding their view of postwar industrial relations. This statement, as its full title and subtitle suggest, appeared to be conciliatory: *INDUSTRIAL PEACE: Progress Report on behalf of the 36 business men who represented American management at the President's Labor-Management Conference, November 5–30, 1945. This report is issued to promote better understanding of the areas of agreement and of disagreement with labor delegates developed at that meeting.*[14]

In this joint 1945 report, as in the proceedings of the Labor-Management Conference itself, business gave no hint that it saw political motivation behind the postwar strike wave. One sees no questioning of labor's Americanism, its patriotism, or its good citizenship. However, by mid 1946, the political climate in general, as well as internal CIO and UAW-CIO developments (discussed in Chapters 4 and 5), once more encouraged the NAM and some of its activist members, notably the Allis-Chalmers Company, to evoke such traditional camouflage language for the purpose of both defeating some strikes and impressing on congressional campaigners the need to curb labor.

While avoiding a head-on clash over collective bargaining, the two leading business organizations, the NAM and the Chamber of Commerce of the United States, had in place their own time-worn Red-based media plans and national political networks for a campaign to roll back the collective power accumulated by unions since the 1930s. On the labor side, traditional AFL/CIO rivalry and new factionalism within the CIO, and perhaps awareness of the Truman administration's offish position on strikes, prevented a

---

[13]CIO Executive Board, minutes, November 1945, p. 3.
[14]National Association of Manufacturers, printed booklet (New York, 1945). The booklet was issued on behalf of both the NAM and the Chamber of Commerce of the United States.

comparable sense of purpose. Instead, new and extraneous political events aggravated internal labor differences and furthered the corporate postwar strategy.

The Changing Government Role

Despite the evolution of federal intervention under the New Deal and during World War II, as well as the General Motors settlement under a Truman-sponsored federal fact-finding formula in early 1946, the Truman administration was showing doubts about retaining the New Deal's basic postwar labor law for postwar labor relations.

We have also seen the strong suspicions Truman held about some union leaders and the strong personal antipathy he had toward leaders he associated with strikes. In the eyes of politically active labor leaders and staffers, Truman was above all a Democratic politician. Labor leaders of all political persuasions feared Harry Truman would not, and could not, ignore the possible political consequences of the postwar strike wave. As previously indicated, however, even those who were fearful about the political consequences of stoppages went along with and even led many of them.

Truman certainly saw nothing positive in the stoppages. Labor in general understood, first, that he was leading the Democrats in an alliance with some key Republicans, notably Senator Arthur Vandenberg of Michigan; second, that the Republicans were making political capital out of the wave of stoppages; and finally, that the president feared that the mounting wave of strikes could result in a Republican victory at the polls and control by the GOP of the 80th Congress. For their part, the Republicans were not at all ambivalent. We – labor lobbyists generally – knew in the early months of 1946 that GOP strategists were pressing in Congress for labor-law changes, associating the wave of strikes publicly with the New Deal and the CIO. The Wagner Act had to go, industrialists in 1945 had agreed. In 1946–7 the GOP concurred, partly because of public antipathy to the strike wave, partly because of the Cold War as it was emerging under President Truman.

As a Senate cloakroom habitué, Truman was quite aware that many of his fellow Democrats in the House and Senate were itching to separate themselves from all traces of the New Deal, especially the Wagner Act. Finally, the president was being daily reminded of some things he knew from his recently concluded Labor-Management Conference: (1) that the Democrats' presumed ally, labor, was divided on the Wagner Act; (2) that industry in its entirety was unwilling to continue that New Deal statute.

While the executive branch of government was wavering, government-appointed fact finders reported that General Motors could pay an 18.5-cent-per-hour increase, and this formula was accepted by the CIO unions' Big Three, the Auto Workers, the Electrical Workers, and the Steel Workers.[15] In some CIO sectors, however, the president was ready to crack down. In my syndicated column of December 20, 1946, I pointed out to my labor readers that the Truman administration was viewing the mere possibility of a maritime left-led strike as a threat against the government. In short, while it was clear that the federal government was going to continue expanding its role in labor relations, labor's role was uncertain, and the direction of intervention under Truman and the postwar legislative branch was by no means defined.

We had decidedly mixed signals from the executive branch. The president and his new secretary of labor, Lewis B. Schwellenbach, justified the demand of labor for higher hourly rates. They also forcefully expressed the right of labor to engage in collective bargaining. On the other hand, the president saw Vandenberg as the key to winning over the Republicans for the forging of a bipartisan coalition in support of the emerging Truman Doctrine, his much higher priority.

At the same time as the Department of Labor was calmly accepting strikes as part of the bargaining process, the president was making strong statements against strikes and voicing annoyance with labor leaders he associated with strikes. We have seen his curt unpublished comment on UAW-CIO president R. J. Thomas and "his" strikers. We can safely assume that Truman felt even less friendly after "R.J." became director of the Local 248 Allis-Chalmers strike in the summer of 1946. In 1946, also, Truman became so angry over the railroad brotherhoods' decision to strike that he went to Congress to ask for the power to draft railway workers to force them to stay on the job, even though they were adhering strictly to the elaborate prestrike rituals of the Railway Labor Act.

Yet there was continued ambiguity in Truman's labor policy. He showed no taste for using bayonets to mine coal. After seizing the coal mines to prevent a stoppage by John L. Lewis, he accepted from his mines administrator, Julius Krug, an agreement that gave the Mine Workers an unprecedented, company-financed welfare pension plan – the first industry-wide "welfare" system in the United States. Finally, the president showed his ambivalence on labor matters by vetoing the Case bill (opposed by the AFL and the CIO), which

[15]The final GM-UAW settlement was for a 17.4-cent increase.

proposed a prestrike fact-finding arrangement similar to his own proposal for fact-finding legislation (also opposed by the AFL and the CIO).

As tensions grew at home and abroad, Truman clearly shifted his views and priorities. The French, Greek, and Italian labor movements were becoming more aggressive. The conflicts with the USSR grew. To many people, war seemed inevitable. Whereas foreign affairs became and remained throughout these first postwar years the predominant interest of Truman, the *New York Times* and other influential publications editorialized that the 1946 stoppages showed that labor was too arrogant and too powerful. The president was voicing similar views in interviews. This was reciprocated. Early in 1946 there was still an increasing alienation from the president among labor leaders. There was a distinct tendency, encouraged by Murray, among CIO leaders to distance themselves from Truman. Often clearing their moves with Philip Murray, CIO lobbyists began to seek out maverick members of Congress, those outside the establishment in the House and Senate.

In a diary note of May 20, 1946, regarding Senator Case's bill, I made no mention of Harry Truman, although I had in the past persistently identified him as a New Dealer, a friend of labor. We – the left and many centrists – simply had no faith now in this president's liberalism, even in his attitude toward Senator Case's fact-finding bill, which he eventually did veto. We felt he was wavering on the right to strike. We therefore pushed our own plans for campaigning against Case's bill. In the diary note, I refer to meetings with three senators on the bill: George D. Aiken, Claude Pepper, and James Murray. Aiken, the Vermont liberal Republican and ranking minority member on the Senate Labor and Public Welfare Committee, had been exposing the NAM for its expensive "educational" campaigns, and we felt he was a more reliable ally than the Democratic floor leader, Alben Barkley (D. Ky.), on the Case bill. Claude Pepper, the most militant of the old New Deal Democrats in the Senate and member of the Labor and Public Welfare Committee, was unsparing in his criticisms of Truman on labor and other domestic matters, and was publicly concerned that war with the Soviet Union might be the result of Truman's foreign policies. I refer to Pepper as "the hero" because of his going to a radio network and giving a "brilliant, off-the-cuff analysis" immediately after the president's call for congressional action to draft the railroad workers and break their announced strike. (This strike was actually called off by the railway brotherhoods before Truman completed his speech to Congress. His legal assistant, the New Dealish Clark Clifford, so notified the president. But the president, evidently caught up in his own rhetoric and the warm response he was getting from Congress, proceeded with his strikebreaking legislative proposal. Even most of the pro-labor members of the House rushed into a stampede for enactment of the president's bill.[16] James Murray was a wealthy, aging Democrat from Montana, who had distanced himself from the White House in taking leadership against the Case bill within the Senate Labor and Welfare Committee, on the floor of the Senate, and in strategy sessions with me and other labor lobbyists.

Whatever the views of Truman and others, the 1946 strikes continued to mount not only in numbers but in man-hours lost. While the Bureau of Labor Statistics calmly tallied the numbers, the administration was becoming nervous. The United States was trying to stop strikes abroad as part of the unfolding Truman Doctrine. Truman and his new secretary of state, James Byrnes of South Carolina, the cabinet, and the president's advisers may have known about the BLS statistics on strike volume and strike causes. They were much more interested in and alarmed, however, by events abroad. As the media and the administration banged away on the new menace, even American labor officials became alarmed. Foreign-policy considerations now had to be taken into account along with domestic questions. On the same day that I wrote my diary notes on the meetings with Aiken, Pepper, and Murray, I indirectly noted the growing isolation of the left: "Things are in horrible shape. Byrnes and Vandenberg dragging us into war, headlines beating steady drumbeat of hate against Russia."[17] And as a reflection of labor's defensiveness, I wrote, "Anti-labor bills being passed, price control being crippled."

But the strike specter wouldn't go away. Even Senator Murray, although alienated from Truman and the official Democratic leadership in the Senate, voiced concern that some of the actual and threatened strikes – justified or not – were encouraging business' drive to change the labor law. I added in my diary note on this interview with the liberal senator from Montana: "Jim Murray thought the railroad unions shouldn't have struck." In retrospect, I

[16]Barton J. Bernstein, ed., *Politics and Policies of the Truman Administration* (Chicago: Quadrangle, 1970), passim. I recall a conversation I had at this time with Representative Herman Koppelman, a one-term liberal Democrat from Connecticut whom I had gotten to know well by 1946. I stopped him at the doorway to the House floor immediately after the House voted to adopt Truman's bill. "Herman, I was surprised to see that you voted for this. It looked like a fascist action," I said. Koppelman replied, roughly as follows: "Irv, I'm a Jew and you know I'm pro-labor. But nobody could have stood up in that atmosphere and voted against the president."

[17]In the diary note I quote Pepper on Byrnes, the secretary of state, who had been the president's chief adviser on reconversion problems, with an office at the White House: "Byrnes doesn't like labor. How can you expect him to like Communists in Russia?" Cf. Walter Isaacson and Evan Thomas, *The Wise Men* (New York: Simon & Schuster, 1986), p. 373, for Truman's and his chief adviser's views in 1946.

must regard it as possible that Senator Murray was conveying a message to me as a CIO representative that the CIO was becoming a scapegoat for antilabor members on both sides of the aisle.

While both the AFL and the independent railroad brotherhoods were as deeply involved in strikes, it was the CIO-type strikes that were attracting political lightning. CIO-affiliated unions had not only voluntarily adopted a no-strike pledge, as had the AFL unions at the onset of the Second World War, but had been an acknowledged major factor in the winning of the war. But when the first round of peacetime strikes began, the CIO industrial-type locals walked out, as did many others, but usually in far greater numbers. Although CIO members were generally striking defensively to enforce either government-approved wartime security arrangements or the postwar wage-adjustment formula to keep up with price increases, or both, some CIO-led strikes, especially those in locals led by communists, did become scapegoats. The Bureau of Labor Statistics, which did not feel it relevant to go into the Red issue or other political issues in its strike analyses, did note that a handful of the 1946 strikes added "unusually high idleness" totals to the aggregate of "work stoppage idleness." Such stoppages, the BLS reported, were more noticeable because they usually involved a greater volume of "work-stoppage idleness (*i.e.*, they involved more workers and were longer, on the average, than in the preceding period) rather than [representing] a substantial increase in the number of stoppages."[18]

The Local 248 strike was long and costly – and was defeated. Local 248 also had a highly visible CP-influenced leadership, a common phenomenon when a union faced a tough corporate employer. The Allis-Chalmers Company not only had a motive but now had an effective public-relations tool for crushing its militant union. It was an NAM activist firm with access to NAM experts apart from its own acquired skill in anti-unionism politics and public relations. It not only effectively utilized the media in Milwaukee for an old-style attack against unionism but showed an ability to exploit new fissures within the CIO. It illustrated those skills by helping to develop a long series of articles in 1946 in the Milwaukee Hearst daily, the *Sentinel*, and then, even more effectively, presenting them to Congress in 1947. Ironically, the company was itself encouraging some "communist dominated" unions in its outlying plants, apparently to undermine the more powerful UAW at West Allis. It made great use of the Red issue, charging in the press and before Congress that Local 248 was so radical that even past and present UAW-CIO and CIO

[18]U.S. Department of Labor, "Postwar Work Stoppages."

leaders were appalled by it. The company settled its 1946 strikes with the Farm Equipment Workers and the United Electrical Workers in its branch plants with only a little delay. But the prolonged strike at West Allis was not settled until after UAW-CIO Local 248 was mercilessly scapegoated at the Taft-Hartley hearings in 1947.

The real difference between the branch plants and the Local 248 situation at the flagship plant was not ideological or political.[19] The company executives responsible for labor policy, and the media they influenced, knew not only that the West Allis local was historically radical but that the current factionalism in the UAW could be profitably politicized. The factional fight in the international UAW-CIO, coming to a climax in 1946–7, offered the company a splendid opportunity to win a major union ally in the old but heretofore unsuccessful desire of the company to destroy its major union at West Allis. The new international president, Walter P. Reuther, was an open foe of the local leaders; he was officially supporting the strike but was known to be opposed to it in practice. In addition, CIO president Philip Murray was also wavering in his support of this particular strike and remaining aware of the growing hostility to CIO strikes in general. Murray was not only responding to some outside pressures but also as an organization man was adjusting to the successful thrust of the right inside his largest affiliate based on the Association of Catholic Trade Unionists' years of work and crowned by the election of Reuther to the UAW-CIO presidency in 1946. The Allis-Chalmers strike at West Allis was actually becoming a test of strength both between management and labor and between the left and right within the CIO itself. Taking his seat on the CIO executive board, Walter Reuther became a very forceful voice of the now aggressive right wing. CIO president Murray was also confronted by additional, if more subtle, pressure from the Truman administration, from virtually all of the media, and from a growing number of politicians, including heretofore pro-union members of Congress.

As the strike wave continued in 1946, one heard Murray expressing in private conversation his own personal trinity. Along with "my union," he was wont to mention more often than in the early years of his presidency "my country" and "my church." This was not mere hyperbole.

The Roman Catholic Church was intimately involved with the CIO and

---

[19]"It is my strong opinion that the Company was not the slightest bit concerned about the Communist question, but rather in a weak and divided labor movement. They actively and openly supported the [Farm Equipment Workers] in Springfield" (letter dated December 4, 1985, to Irving Richter from Marshall Hughes, former Allis-Chalmers employee at Springfield, Mo., and UAW member).

with Murray, as indeed it had been with the older American Federation of Labor. In the pre-CIO era, when the Socialist Party was a force in U.S. unions, the Church had developed its own caucuses to limit labor's involvement to business unionism – what Lenin once contemptuously called "economism" and the AFL hierarchy proudly termed "pure and simple" unionism. With the coming of the CIO, the Church began exerting pressure on Murray and other leaders of the CIO through the Association of Catholic Trade Unionists to oust the communist left. In 1946, also, the archdiocese of New York, under Francis Cardinal Spellman, as employer of CIO-organized striking Cemetery Workers and unorganized office workers, was not only ideologically concerned but pressing Murray to step in against the bargaining demands of two left-wing unions representing those workers in the New York area.[20] As is often the case, the Church interest was interlocked with the flag. And, as we have already noted, the government as well as the flag of the United States was inextricably linked with the industrial unions' unfinished organizing tasks.

Under Lewis, as under Murray, organizers and local leaders of the CIO had consistently and prominently displayed American flags on their picket lines and in victory parades. The flag signified an appreciation that the federal government had legitimized the new unions' organizing plans (and strikes when necessary) to penetrate basic industry. During the war, the CIO was as patriotic as any institution. After the war, Murray continued to feel the ongoing CIO need for presidential friendship and assistance. Thus, while Murray encouraged Hillman to proceed with independent liberal coalition building, he was not about to break with the White House. In this light, his proclaiming of Church and country was related to his more publicized "resent and resist" position at the 1946 convention. This speech resulted in a resolution signaling

---

[20]Murray papers, Catholic University of America, box 27. The strike question and associated organizing problems were alluded to in memorandum written – possibly dictated by Murray – in Washington, D.C., apparently to make sure Murray saw the file in Pittsburgh, where he spent much time on steel-union matters. These memoranda make reference to both phone calls and visits to Murray by a representative of the New York archdiocese. As a result of the calls and visits, Murray agreed to send no less a personage than Allen Haywood, the CIO's national director of organization, to look into the strike by the Cemetery Workers and the organizing plans of the office workers in the archdiocese. The strike was led by the National Food and Tobacco Workers of America (FTA), and the organizing was being done by the United Office and Professional Workers of America (UOPWA), both leading left-wing affiliates. They would be among the eleven national unions expelled by the CIO in 1949 on charges of "communist domination." I do not know the results of Haywood's trip from any written documentation. I am of the opinion (partly from a 1980 interview with Elizabeth Sasuly, the former FTA Washington representative) that the strike was called off and the organizational efforts halted at least partly as a result of the Church's intervention.

the CIO's distancing itself from the communist left. Conventionally and accurately viewed as a disavowal of communist influence in the CIO, that resolution can also be interpreted as a move by Murray to keep the CIO in step with President Truman; specifically, to show sympathy with the president's anxiety about communism in order to retain White House and Democratic Party help. Whether or not it mollified the White House, the CIO 1946 convention declaration marked the beginning of the end of independent political action and the onset of a new and intensified alliance with the Democratic Party. But while increasing his presence in the Democratic Party and therefore within the administration, Murray carefully and deliberately refrained from using his expanded White House influence to help salvage the now highly politicized losing strike at West Allis.

The UAW-Murray Nexus

The international union formally entitled Automobile, Aircraft, and Agricultural Workers of America was an autonomous CIO affiliate whose president sat on the CIO executive board. The UAW authorized its own strikes. Thus, the UAW-CIO international executive board on March 31, 1946, authorized the Local 248 stoppage of work, along with many other round-one strikes. One must consider the factional situation in the UAW to fully grasp the political consequences – not causes – of that strike. Walter Reuther was now president, having defeated Murray's friend, the avowedly anticommunist centrist R. J. Thomas at the 1946 convention of the Auto Workers. While Reuther automatically became the UAW's representative on the CIO executive board, "the Redhead" was still embattled with what he called the "mechanical majority" of his own international executive board. Without a board majority, he could not control the organization. The board meetings continued to authorize stoppages in 1946 and 1947. They hinted at dissent, however, over the Allis-Chalmers Local 248 strike.

All through 1946, tensions within the CIO and especially in the UAW-CIO grew far more than the record suggests, particularly after many round-two strikes were authorized in the summer of 1946; but the Allis-Chalmers round-one strike remained unsettled. As one may readily gather from the Allis-Chalmers Company testimony at the Taft-Hartley House hearings (see Chapter 4), this corporation was remaining firm against the local's demands, partly because of the CIO president's growing disenchantment with the left within the entire CIO and, even more significant, the split within the UAW board over this stoppage by one of its most militant and one of the auto union's Red

locals. The UAW-CIO international executive board minutes suggest but minimize the actual charges and countercharges between the new president and
the majority anti-Reuther group on the board.

As we have seen, the "mechanical majority" of the board was led by R. J.
Thomas and George F. Addes. On the issue of the strike by Local 248, Joseph
Mattson, the regional director for Illinois-Wisconsin, who had joined the
Thomas-Addes caucus, linked his defense of the strike with criticism not only
of Allis-Chalmers but also of President Reuther, whom he frequently accused
(in off-the-record comments at and outside board meetings) of paying mere lip
service to the strike while joining in the Red-baiting orchestrated by the
company and the Milwaukee *Sentinel*.

Both Mattson and Vice-President Thomas frequently hinted at factional
motivations among the Reuther group. But this was a two-sided factional
fight. Thomas and Addes and other centrists were themselves at least partly
motivated by internal politics. The *Sentinel* and the company both took note
of the fact that Thomas as president had himself voiced criticism of the
Communist Party influence in Local 248. The firm's chief labor specialist
would reiterate his own distaste for communism at the congressional hearings
in 1947 and also cite these internal conflicts. Thomas would then appear as a
defender of the local and its strikes. At least in part, his switch in sympathies
came about because he was dependent on the left for whatever future he might
have in the UAW-CIO. Mattson, a centrist now allied with Thomas, had also
made his career in the Auto Workers dependent on the large and disciplined
block of votes of this left-wing local. He well knew that Local 248 had
supported him in his reelection as regional director in 1946 and could defeat
him and Thomas at the upcoming Reuther-chaired 1947 convention.

One finds no hint in the UAW board minutes of the role played by Phil
Murray. Although the CIO president was withdrawing from the traditional
left-center CIO coalition, he was still uncommitted in the UAW-CIO factional
fight. He still maintained great influence among all officers. And both factions were now courting him. But neither the right nor the left was prepared to
openly test Phil Murray's personal loyalties. Yet by his refusal to act personally on behalf of the seizure of Allis-Chalmers, a key demand of the now
desperate local, Murray showed that he was moving off center and to the
right. He was still maintaining his old friendship with Thomas, the ex-welder
at Chrysler who was now a vice-president of the UAW-CIO and the most
publicized opponent of President Walter Reuther. At the June 1946 meeting of
the UAW board, Thomas had been designated director of the Allis-Chalmers
strike in Wisconsin. Although the local officers agreed to this action with

alacrity, it was an implicit sign of the international's lack of full confidence in the local leadership. But despite his warm personal feelings for R. J. Thomas and his distaste for Walter Reuther, and despite the board's vote for seizure, Murray was not giving his personal support to that demand of the Allis-Chalmers strikers.

The strike dragged on. The rank and file, as in their struggles against the company in earlier periods, were apparently ready to continue to make sacrifices to save their workplace organization. But the local was facing political changes not only in the international union and in the CIO but in Wisconsin as well. In the original 1937 organizing of the huge plant at West Allis, the workers seeking to unionize had had not only the aid of a friendly White House and a National Labor Relations (Wagner) Act, but also a decidedly pro-union "Little Wagner Act" passed by the Wisconsin legislature. In the aftermath of the 1939 victory of the Republican Party, the Allis-Chalmers Company had helped draft and enact a revision of the Wisconsin act to give the state authority to act against "strike violence." Following some picket-line violence after a back-to-work movement begun by Allis-Chalmers management in October 1946, the company requested and won from the reconstructed Wisconsin Employment Relations Board a decertification election. Despite months of deprivation and adverse publicity, that election resulted in a slim majority vote for retention of the existing local. The local, of course, claimed with some validity that this majority vote meant that the rank and file favored continuation of the strike at West Allis.

Certainly the workers at West Allis and elsewhere were aware that some local leaders were Communist Party members. Defiance of the government, however, was not an issue in this strike, any more than it was in the vast majority of 1945–6 stoppages.[21] Neither this local nor its members were advocating revolution. Indeed, despite the vast outpouring of political publicity about the walkout by the local and by the media, this prolonged strike was in fact defensive and apolitical. Its unusual duration was primarily a function of the firm's refusal to accept government standards of wages and union security.

By the fall of 1946, the great strike wave had crested. The BLS had shown no significant political coordination or causation in the stoppages. Most

---

[21] For a more class-oriented interpretation of the postwar strike wave, see Jeremy Brecher, *Strike! The True History of Mass Insurgence in America from 1877 to the Present – As Authentic Revolutionary Movements Against the Establishments of State, Capital, and Trade Unionism* (San Francisco: Straight Arrow, 1973), pp. 227–30. Brecher stresses instances where rank-and-file solidarity cut across institutional lines.

strikes were settled after relatively short shutdowns over purely economic issues. But there was a distinct political backlash against organized labor over the unprecedented number of strikes. Only a few were prolonged stoppages. An unknown, but distinctly small, total were led by communists and other radicals. However, the Republican Party opposition – long denied power in Washington – seized on the wave of strikes, and on the Local 248 strike in particular, to renew its long-term hostility to the New Deal. In a thinly disguised attack on existing labor law, the GOP evolved for its congressional campaign of 1946 the promise of combating "Communism, Chaos, and Confusion." The new chairpersons of the congressional labor committees, Representative Hartley and Senator Taft, proceeded to reverse the basic labor law, receiving significant help from Allis-Chalmers Company executives, the National Association of Manufacturers, and Democratic politicians.

4

THE TAFT-HARTLEY LEGISLATIVE
SCENE

The Labor-Management Relations (Taft-Hartley) Act of 1947 is frequently treated, even by experts, as a continuation of Wagner Act policy. Insofar as Taft-Hartley accepted collective bargaining, there was a continuity. However, Taft-Hartley, which would further fragment the already divided labor movement, was a very basic shift in federal labor policy.

Whereas Section 7 of the Wagner Act had provided a straightforward, protected right of employees to join unions and bargain collectively, Taft-Hartley shifted the basis of labor law from this protected right of employees to protection of the right *not* to join unions and *not* to bargain. This change – buttressed by many other new provisions designed to split labor and limit free bargaining or directly help employers – had then and continues to have decisive effects on all collective bargaining.

A recent authority, James A. Gross, professor of industrial and labor relations at Cornell University, has analyzed in his valuable book the transition in national labor policy. Gross has also argued, in an article written after several years of much-publicized malaise in the labor movement, that confusion in national policy results partly from the contradictions about purpose in the 1947 act. He maintains that in the final conference version Representative Hartley's wish to deny collective bargaining altogether is represented, along with the original Wagner Act's purpose of encouraging collective bargaining.[1]

I have previously discussed several Taft-Hartley provisions that I considered a reversal of Wagner Act protections: the right-to-work Section 14(b), which expressly permitted the states to bar union security clauses, and the

---

[1]James A. Gross, *The Reshaping of the National Labor Relations Board: National Labor Policy in Transition, 1937–1947* (Albany: Press of the State University of New York, 1981). In a 1985 article, Gross states that "Congress legislated contradictory statutory purposes into the Taft-Hartley Act, so that after 50 years our national labor policy is at cross-purposes with itself." Gross refers to the "purpose" in the preambles of the two statutes ("Conflicting Statutory Purposes: Another Look at 50 Years of the NLRB Law Making," *Industrial and Labor Relations Review*, 39, no. 1 [October 1985]: 7–34).

section barring supervisory employees. In an earlier study, I dwelled on Section 8(b)(4), the anti–secondary-boycott provision, which I then believed was mainly directed against the traditional practices of the AFL-affiliated building-craft unions seeking control of the better-paying jobs in construction.[2]

This was true. But Section 8(b)(4) and (7) also retarded organization of industrial unions. Eugene Cotton, veteran general counsel of the CIO-affiliated United Packinghouse Workers (UPWA), notes that Section 8(b) in the CIO packinghouse union "virtually eliminated strikes for union recognition"; that it also meant

> that UPWA could not picket the butcher stores and supermarkets and other wholesale and retail outlets of unbranded products of struck plants, and UPWA members in those establishments could not support the strike by refusing to handle the products, that UPWA workers in plants supplying the struck plant were forced to scab on their fellow union members because they could not refuse to work on products being sent into the struck plant. The introduction of the entire body of union unfair labor practices in Section 8(b) (consistent with the "balanced" revision of Section 7) meant in effect that the shield of protection of employee rights under the Wagner Act was reversed to become, instead, a line of cannons pointed against labor.[3]

According to Cotton, the injunction provisions of Taft-Hartley had severely damaging effects on all unions, but were "devastatingly evil" as implemented against the relatively low-paid, largely unskilled employees in packing: "And the anti-labor provisions in T/H [notwithstanding the 1931 Norris–La Guardia anti-injunction law] were to be enforced not merely by the long drawn-out procedure of complaint hearing . . . but, far more devastatingly, by virtually mandatory, quickly issued court injunctions against unions."[4]

The labor movement was highly ambivalent about the bills and the final conference version that became the new federal law. It was not prepared politically or psychologically to resist an assault on its gains. But the change from the New Deal's basic labor law, the Wagner Act, was neither the "slave-labor" law of union rhetoric nor the "bill of rights" that Taft and Hartley

---

[2]Irving Richter, *Political Purpose in Trade Unions* (London: Allen & Unwin, 1973), ch. 10. The AFL and later the AFL-CIO did indeed make repeal of the "situs picketing" ban – as Section 8(b)(4) was termed by the construction unions – the top priority in legislative goals after the U.S. Supreme Court in 1951 definitively ruled that such secondary picketing was a violation of the secondary-boycott provision and should therefore be enjoined.

[3]Letter from Cotton, January 3, 1988, pp. 2–3, commenting on a draft of this book. Cotton was formerly associate general counsel, CIO, the legislative specialist. He left the national CIO in 1946 when he was appointed general counsel of the United Packinghouse Workers of America by Helstein. I return to the UPWA in Chapter 5.

[4]Ibid., p. 4.

claimed it to be. Under the restrictions of Taft-Hartley, the unions knew they could continue to function. And they did. Despite a shift to the right, this was a period of continued "welfare-state" reforms, with society committed to high employment and growth of production. Once it became clear that there would be no depression after World War II, as many had expected, labor leaders envisaged the postwar period as one in which they would hold onto wartime gains and use their strength to make new economic and political gains.

However, while elements of the welfare state were maintained, Truman's Democratic administration, the opposition Republicans, the Dixiecrats, and the media were now in effect united in seeking to root out radicalism. Representative Hartley and a few diehards openly opposed collective bargaining altogether. But in practice the opposition to unions took the form of opposing strikes, and particularly "political" strikes – this becoming the accepted terminology for strikes led by communists, suspected communists, or fellow travelers.

By 1947, most national leaders were fully aware of altered public opinion: a steady shift against unions and union leaders at every level. In this new political environment, internal union politics also shifted. The leadership felt they had to prove they were patriotic and hence at least noncommunist, or, better yet, anticommunist and antiradical. This led them to accept and promote affidavit signing and compliance.

The historic strike wave of 1946 was over by 1947. The 1946 congressional elections had signaled a national readiness for sociopolitical change and a receptiveness to casting strikes and stoppages in terms of anticommunism. The Republicans had won control of the 80th Congress largely by identifying themselves with the national interest: not specifically against labor, but against strikes. The abbreviated version of their 1946 congressional campaign theme had been the "Three C's: Communism, Confusion and Chaos." Concealing more than it illuminated, and endorsed by most of the media and some leaders of labor, that simple electoral slogan succeeded by promising that everything would be all right if only subversives were eliminated. Once again, as in past labor crises, the complexities of industrial relations were simply swept under the carpet.

In 1947, the new Republican-led Congress began its assault on labor law. Guided by volunteer corporate lawyers and older opponents of the New Deal, the leadership of the 80th Congress adhered to and implemented the GOP campaign slogan, first when they organized the committee structure, and second when determining legislative strategies. Since the Truman White House was not committed to prevailing labor law, the Wagner Act had few committee defenders, even among Democrats. The strike specter remained a vivid one for corporate America, for the Truman administration, and for the GOP. An additional perceived danger was that an important segment of labor – the CIO, which had been acting since 1943 as an independent political force – was still relatively united.

The strike specter stressed by Truman and Vandenberg in 1945 now swayed the legislators. Although by early 1947 a settlement had been reached in the vast majority of disputes, a few remained unsettled. One of these unsettled strikes, the one at the West Allis plant of Allis-Chalmers, had the ingredients necessary for the change in labor law. Accordingly, this labor-management dispute, though typical of postwar stoppages, was politicized and publicized by the Allis-Chalmers management before the hearings and then by the House Committee on Education and Labor (the Hartley Committee) at its hearings. In addition to being facilitated by the favorable political climate for reversing the new labor law, the change was helped along by the much-publicized struggle for power within the Auto Workers union, now more than ever pivotally important for the entire CIO. The newly elected president of that union was prepared to use the strike, and the noncommunist section, to defeat the left-led UAW local and to consolidate his control over the region and the international.

Local 248 of the UAW had been organized in the wave of industrial union-ism. Here, as in many CIO unions and in some AFL "federal" locals, political radicals (often skilled employees with union experience and sometimes still attached to old-line craft unions) became prominent in the leadership. The individuals who managed to outmaneuver the historically anti-union Allis-Chalmers Company and become elected leaders included a corps of radicals – socialists and socialists-turned-communists – who knew how to take advan-tage of state and national labor laws. The State of Wisconsin, deeply influ-enced by La Follette progressivism since the turn of the century, had produced a strong Socialist Party, which split into left and right wings and included a significant Communist Party during the Great Depression. Cadres of both the Socialist and Communist parties helped organize the metalworking industries in the mid 1930s, including Allis-Chalmers, the largest factory in the state.

The CP's role was an accepted political and economic fact of life in the UAW-CIO, the Wisconsin CIO, and the national CIO under Lewis and Mur-ray. But the company, which had tolerated its union in the New Deal and war years, was not interested in sharing power in the postwar period with any independent labor union, let alone a militant and politically radical local of the unpredictable UAW. Allis-Chalmers managers, like many others, were known to favor a union-free workplace. If that was impossible, the company officials wanted a more conservative union leadership.

Whatever the final outcome of the legislation, the company's assault on the Allis-Chalmers strikers was part of a wider corporate attack on Wagner rather than a response to politically caused strikes. The firm had joined earlier employer drives to defeat, amend, and weaken enforcement of the New Deal labor law. However, by 1947 all major union groupings were functioning peacefully and accepting a relatively benign and helpful federal role. Thousands of contracts were in place. The old NLRB was conducting new certification elections, encouraging the signing of contracts, and leaving to the locals the selection of officers. In short, the NLRB was generally enforcing the declared purpose of the original National Labor Relations Act: to encourage collective bargaining without regard to the affiliations or associations of elected leaders.

After many years of bargaining, Allis-Chalmers had accumulated valuable management experience in labor relations. One would have expected an emphasis on that experience before the key congressional committee. Instead, Allis-Chalmers executives testifying before Hartley's committee, having mentioned how "unfair" the existing union contract was to management, focused mainly on the "political" nature of UAW Local 248. The heavy expenditure – for a five-man executive team sent to Washington, and for the voluminous cloth-bound, gold-embossed briefs – was no doubt justified by the ultimate aim of reduction in labor costs. But to achieve that bottom-line goal, the brief and remarks by Allis-Chalmers witnesses were heavily ideological.

Allis-Chalmers management witnesses for Taft-Hartley mirrored and significantly promoted the public obsession with the communist threat at home and abroad. Relying heavily on the Allis-Chalmers case, the labor committee not only adopted Taft-Hartley but also inserted a ban, later ruled unconstitutional, known as the noncommunist affidavit. The new law won quick passage over Truman's veto and quick acceptance by labor and the general public.[5]

The left wing of the CIO was a primary target of Taft-Hartley. Among other contemporary observers, eminent Cambridge University labor historian Henry Pelling, writing in the late 1950s, concurred with what he considered the

---

[5]There are many studies of the legislation. The "bill-of-rights" claim referred to above is in Fred A. Hartley, *Our New Labor Policy* (New York: Funk & Wagnall in association with Modern Industry Magazine, n.d. [apparently published in 1948]), p. 14. (The book has a Foreword by Senator Robert A. Taft.) The AFL executive council, though briefly divided in 1947, signed the affidavits in late 1947 and was upheld by the convention. The CIO, because of Murray's ambivalence, was hesitant at the center, signing in 1949; most affiliated unions, generally with encouragement from the center, decided to sign and comply by 1948.

target of Taft-Hartley: "Communist influence" in the CIO, formed in the "Red decade" of the 1930s. Professor Pelling and others observing labor and U.S. politics at the time emphasized the high relevance of the Red issue not only for Congress in the genesis of Taft-Hartley but in the CIO in the same period. This British observer noted that CIO president Philip Murray had already in 1946 dissociated the CIO from the CPUSA. By the time of Taft-Hartley, the CIO was showing considerable ambivalence. However, the splits widened: "The struggle against the Communists became more acute . . . partly as a result of the anti-Communist provisions of the Taft-Hartley Act."[6]

As Pelling saw it, anti-unionists in Congress in 1947 were capitalizing on the CIO's internal struggles. There is little doubt that what Pelling called the "anti-Communist provisions of the Taft-Hartley Act" aggravated the splits. Indeed, Section 9(h) mesmerized the entire labor movement. (Pelling, it should be noted, used the term "anti-Communist," not "non-Communist," for Section 9(h). He thereby captured the preferred private interpretation of Section 9(h) by many contemporary leaders in Congress and in labor. In public, labor leaders generally chose to use the phrase "noncommunist" or "loyalty.") While established national leaders rushed to sign and comply, the left generally advocated nonsigning and hence noncompliance with Taft-Hartley.

The Allis-Chalmers Corporate Testimony

The Allis-Chalmers case was chosen by the House labor committee and its advisers as a key example of problems to be addressed by new labor legislation. In the remainder of this chapter, I will focus on the Allis-Chalmers corporate testimony and then on evidence offered by auto labor leaders. For this important analysis I rely on my memory and my notes and writings of the time, on the hearings, and on scholarly work.

The portrait of labor relations presented by the battery of five Allis-Chalmers corporate witnesses testifying in Washington on Taft-Hartley in early 1947 was based more on the ideological dogma of the day, anticommunism, than on the history of labor relations at the flagship West Allis, Wisconsin, plant. Company executives charged that Local 248, though affiliated with the UAW and the CIO, originated with the Communist Party and still was dominated by it. The ongoing 1946–7 strike was "political," not a legitimate trade union action. These charges were given respectful credence by the

---

[6]Henry Pelling, *American Labor* (Chicago: University of Chicago Press, 1960), p. 162. Cf. Roger Keeran, *The Communist Party and the Autoworkers' Union* (Bloomington: Indiana University Press, 1980), pp. 270–82.

House Committee on Education and Labor, figured prominently in the questioning and later prosecution of union witnesses, and also became a major argument for the noncommunist-affidavit Section 9(h) of the final Taft-Hartley Act.

Although it was routinely authorized by the UAW international in early 1946, the strike called by Local 248 provided the Republicans with an opportunity once again to advance the Three C's slogan – "Communism, Confusion and Chaos" – that had proven so successful in the 1946 congressional elections. The company now also referred to the ongoing strike, the current conflict between Local 248 and the international president, and past conflicts between the local and top union officers.

While declining in membership as a result of the strike and company resistance, Local 248 had become a factor of internal political importance to the UAW's incumbent president and to his so-called left-wing opposition for control of the UAW. The public was also interested now in this internal struggle because of its key importance for the outcome of the CIO's publicized quarrels.

There was little doubt in the UAW, even before the hearings, that the local was headed by people who, ever since they signed the first 1937 contract, were on the left: either members of the Communist Party or fellow travelers. Many resolutions passed at local membership meetings paralleled the zigs and zags of the Communist Party. The factor of radical politics was indeed present. But now the more important explanatory factor was that the local remained firmly in the Addes-Thomas (center-left) coalition. Although both Addes and Thomas frequently asserted their anti-CP beliefs, this local had become a storm center within the fractious auto union. Both the right and center-left were bidding for its large block of convention votes.

Local 248 was also one of the most prominent targets of the House Committee on Un-American Activities (HUAC) hearings and reports as well as of investigations by the Federal Bureau of Investigation. Soon after passage of Taft-Hartley, the local would be one of the first subjects of a special inquiry by a subcommittee of the House Committee on Education and Labor appointed by Hartley to determine whether the incumbent local leaders should be cited for perjury on a charge of lying about their CP membership before the committee.

In sum, Local 248 was a significant if diminishing radical force in a society rapidly moving to the right. The incumbent UAW top officer, Walter Reuther, as well as the man Reuther defeated in 1946 for the presidency of the international, R. J. Thomas, had in the past charged communist influence in the local. The corporate brief did not specify the political leanings of Philip Murray, CIO president; he was still officially neutral in the Reuther-Thomas rivalry. But he too was moving to the right. Murray had in 1946 rejected overtures from his friend R. J. Thomas, who, though leader of the Allis-Chalmers strike, was now part of the opposition to an important CIO executive board member, Walter Reuther. A clue to Murray's shift was his refusal to intervene on behalf of the union by asking for presidential seizure of the plant. The CIO executive board, which still contained many left-wing union leaders, had unanimously requested such seizure. None of us on the staff were surprised to learn of Murray's de facto dissociation from the strike, since we had seen Murray's steady (albeit ambiguous) dissociation from the left in general. The fact that Local 248 had been for years the largest CIO local in Wisconsin, the backbone of the Milwaukee and Wisconsin CIO, was not decisive in the changing political climate of 1947.

The media were associating Local 248 with the CIO left, although the seizure motion advanced by the local and its supporters showed a reliance on the Truman administration – still under suspicion within the CIO – and clearly was not a radical impulse. Nevertheless, this local was anathema to Allis-Chalmers. In advance of the key House hearings, the Hearst newspaper chain had sent to all opinion makers, including Murray and all members of Congress, copies of front-page articles from the Milwaukee *Sentinel,* packaged in a bright-red and white hammer-and-sickle cover, "proving" communist domination of the local and of CIO councils in Wisconsin. This could not have been prepared by the *Sentinel* without significant help from the company's management. In this period of fading public support for any cooperation with the left, the old CP-influenced CIO unions were being isolated, not only by the change in the UAW and Philip Murray's own swerving to the right but by political changes at home and abroad. The famous CIO left-wing board members – Harry Bridges, Joe Curran, Abe Flaxer, Ben Gold, and Joe Selly, among others – and the two prominent left-wing staff directors at the national CIO, de Caux and Pressman, were still trying to avoid an open argument or break with Murray, the symbol of the CP's labor-liberal united front: They did not push him to lend his personal support to the strikers.

As for R. J. Thomas, a Murray confidant and a centrist, he often expressed to me and other intimates his estimate that Murray continued to have a personal distaste for "the Redhead," Walter Reuther. Thomas, however, was also aware that since his own defeat by Reuther for the UAW presidency, Murray was "a goner" – that is, he could no longer be counted upon as a keystone for the left-center coalition in the CIO. Indeed, Thomas would soon go to work for the national CIO, hired by Murray, and he repeated that estimate to me before deciding to accept the job.

One should see the withdrawal of Murray from personal support for the Allis-Chalmers strike as a significant signal to Congress that even the relatively progressive CIO would not go out of its way to show support for left-wing unionism.[7]

Representative Hartley and his colleagues were very warm toward Allis-Chalmers witnesses. A conspicuously cooler and decidedly more political reception was given the union's case. This unusual behavior, again, reflected the times. Bipartisanship on foreign policy notwithstanding, Hartley, like other GOP leaders, was on the offensive against all domestic laws associated with the fading New Deal and the New Deal's strongest ally, the CIO. The Committee on Un-American Activities was now enjoying higher funding and greater prestige under Representative J. Parnell Thomas, its new Republican chairman. While continuing the familiar and largely bipartisan HUAC investigations, invariably showing that the CIO and New Deal agencies were "communist-dominated," this committee had gone to Hollywood for a sensational, highly publicized investigation. That investigation led to the motion picture industry's famous blacklist under which jobs were lost and housing, schooling, and even the very lives of employees and their families were endangered. As scholars of the period have noted, HUAC, as well as FBI investigations of the CIO and independent unions in the motion picture industry, along with media sensationalism, had a powerful effect in shifting the climate of public opinion against liberalism and radicalism.[8]

[7]Although Len deCaux was dropped by Murray and replaced by a self-styled right-wing editor and publicist, Allen Swim, the CIO continued to show many pre–New Deal tendencies in its press and in other actions. See Chapter 5.

[8]David Wise, *The Government Against the People: The American Police State* (New York: Random House, 1976); Eric F. Goldman, *The Crucial Decade and After: America, 1945–60* (New York: Knopf, 1984); Frank Donner, *The Age of Surveillance* (New York: Knopf, 1984); Arthur Kinoy, *Rights on Trial* (Cambridge, Mass.: Harvard University Press, 1983); David Caute, *The Great Fear: The Anti-Communist Purge Under Truman and Eisenhower* (New York: Simon & Schuster, 1986), pp. 253–439.

Sam Kushner, *The Long Road to Delano* (New York: International Publishers, 1975), shows the effect of "anticommunist terror" in the 1920s and 1930s in the organizing of California migrant agricultural workers. More recently, Ann Fagan Ginger and David Christiano (*The Cold War Against Labor* [Berkeley, Calif.: Meiklejohn Civil Liberties Institute, 1987]) edited a two-volume, left-oriented anthology covering the period from 1946 through the 1950s, focusing on the CIO internal purge, the impact of Taft-Hartley and subsequent acts of Congress, and vindication-of-the-left decisions by the U.S. Supreme Court. Junius Irving Scales and Richard Nickson (*Cause at Heart* [Athens: University of Georgia Press, 1987]) have an interesting and valuable legal and constitutional commentary by Telford Taylor, as well as Scales' own observations of what he calls "anti-communist apparently unanswerable arguments" during the 1948–56 post–Taft-Hartley period in Winston Salem and other industrial centers in North Carolina. Scales, who had been a full-time CP official in North Carolina, was arrested and brought to trial under the 1940 Smith Act, *after* he had left the CPUSA.

The Republican majority on the labor committee adopted a strange standard of conduct. Although it fuddled the issue of labor relations and was one-sided and prejudiced, it found the old smokescreen of antiradicalism, now expressed as anticommunism, to be an approved form of legislative discourse. In the political climate of the day, which the committee sensed, all one had to do to win approval was to uncover a Red plot. The labor people, center, left, and right, all recognized this as a new fact of political life. But very few, even among CP-influenced unions, were willing to stand up for the constitutional rights of people accused of being communists or fellow travelers. All this was of course a source of pleasure for industrialists opposing labor's role in postwar America.

Chairman Hartley, as George Meany recalled later, had decided that in the new environment he could "do better for himself by linking himself with industry, even at the cost of giving up his old friendship with the American Federation of Labor."[9] Meany also noted that in selecting Hartley as chairman the Republicans slid around the unwritten seniority rule, jumping over a Republican liberal, Richard A. Welsh.[10] The majority party, and the minority opposition as well, also ignored a general contempt on Capitol Hill toward Hartley for incompetence and lack of fairness.

His predecessor, long-standing chairperson Representative Mary T. Norton (D., N.J.), instead of quietly taking her place as ranking minority member after the Republican sweep of 1946, took the unusual step of resigning from the committee. Norton charged publicly that Mr. Hartley had attended only six meetings during the ten years she chaired the labor committees, and stated further, "I have no respect for the present Chairman of the Labor Committee." Whatever his personal limitations, opportunism, and prior lack of interest, Chairman Hartley received expert guidance. I noted at the time that this help came not only from Democratic and Republican colleagues but also from industry experts assigned to the committee by the Allis-Chalmers Company and the National Association of Manufacturers.[11] I also noted that corporate lawyers attended executive sessions and public meetings of the committee, openly guided Hartley, organized the questioning of witnesses, and helped draft reports.[12]

---

[9]Archie Robinson, *George Meany and His Times* (New York: Simon & Schuster, 1981), pp. 144–5. Meany based his judgment on interviews with Hartley in 1947.
[10]Ibid., p. 144.
[11]Irving Richter, "Behind Washington Headlines: Dirty Work Behind Closed Doors," *Headlight* (Buick Local 599, UAW-CIO), April 15, 1947. My sources inside the committee were Democratic members and permanent staffers. Cf. Hartley, *Our New Labor Policy,* passim. See also Bert Cochran (below, n. 30).
[12]Irving Richter, Richter Exposes Masters of Rep. Hartley," *Ford Facts,* April 26, 1947, p. 1.

The communism part of the Republicans' three C's campaign slogan was well established. The confusion and chaos parts were registered in the public mind in 1946. Now the company hammered away at the three C's by identifying the strike at West Allis as political. In reality, according to the old NAM argument, all strikes were unnecessary. Harold W. Story, an attorney as well as a vice-president and chief labor-relations officer, now argued that his company's flagship plant stoppages of production resulted from and also led to a communist "menace" and to the very chaos and confusion that American society had voted against in 1946. The clear intent and effect of the extended Allis-Chalmers phase of the hearings was to push along restrictions on all forms of unionism. By focusing, however, on the importance of denying communists access to the Labor Board, the corporation hoped to isolate Reds from the rest of labor and shift the union's concern from their adherence to collective bargaining to an active involvement in society's struggle against the "menace."

One of the most remarkable features of these Allis-Chalmers hearings, by far the most extensive of any company-union relationship the committee considered, is that the cause of the long 1946–7 strike was given virtually no serious attention. The members of this congressional committee, known in the past for fairness and thoroughness, now preferred to paint a political portrait consistent with popular imagery. The members did have a few procedural and substantive conflicts. There was a minority report signed by five Democrats against some features of the conference bill, H.R. 3020. But the committee achieved unanimity in its denunciation of the strike weapon. All seemed to agree, moreover, that this particular strike by one relatively obscure local was associated with the worldwide "communist menace."[13]

Story spoke of the abuse of employee representation by local officers, by which he meant denial of members' rights. Both Taft and Hartley later cited

This was based on a special telephoned report by me to the editor of *Ford Facts*, Robert Lieberman. During the preceding week, I opened my labor column by citing Senator Taft's strategy on the Senate side: "The new Taft anti-labor bill means this: the Senator from Ohio has decided to count again on communism, confusion and chaos – the three Cs which won for the Republicans in 1946" ("Inside the Senate Labor and Public Welfare Committee," ibid., April 19, 1947). In actual fact, the Senate bill was far more cautious and moderate in content. The hearings were also decidedly less one-sided, and the conferees the Senate appointed were not as ideologically opposed to unionism as the House conferees. Essentially, Taft's version recognized collective bargaining in principle.

[13]For the general link between attacks on labor and foreign policy, see Ronald Radosh, *American Labor and United States Foreign Policy: The Cold War in the Unions from Gompers to Lovestone* (New York: Random House, 1969). Cf. Serafino Romualdi, "Labor and Democracy in Latin America," *Foreign Affairs*, 25, no. 3 (April 1947): 478–89, for Latin American affairs involving the AFL, its affiliates, and the work of staffers such as Romualde, Lovestone, and the underrated Irving Brown.

that part of Allis-Chalmers' testimony to justify their "bill of rights." This charge of unions' failure to fully represent the interests of all members was by 1947 a well-known fact of industrial life. This failure was especially blatant with regard to African-American members, who were generally denied entrance or promotion to skilled and in some cases even to semiskilled work.[14]

However, notwithstanding Allis-Chalmers' expression of concern for the membership, Story failed to develop relevant evidence on the point either from company or other experience. Instead, the witness gave a traditional corporate rejection of employee efforts to bargain collectively, and a banal justification for the revocation of union security and the unilateral termination of the referee system imposed during the war at West Allis by the National War Labor Board.

Story was of course aware of the two sponsors' bills, and of their differences. Senator Taft was known to be more careful about observing constitutionality, and did not wish to wipe out all traces of collective bargaining. (However, in his foreword to Hartley's 1948 book Taft summarized his own far-reaching objectives: first, "fundamental revision of the Wagner law"; second, "to reduce the arbitrary power of labor leaders"; and third, to curb strikes, which, Taft said, was "one of the issues of the 1946 elections.")[15]

Not only did Story favor Hartley's tougher approach, but his company, an activist firm in the NAM, had a hand in the drafting of the House bill, a fact that I and others reported on extensively at the time. In his summary, Story used the Local 248 stoppage to justify a policy of not settling with union leaders and to simultaneously legitimize his company's back-to-work strategy – a standard employer antistrike technique it was then using at its Wisconsin plant. He also cited the "violent" strike to justify the company's need for "remedial legislation." In the printed brief, the headings for these two points are connected by a headline: "How Allis-Chalmers during the strike met the challenge of communism, by a sound industrial relations policy applying to striker and non-striker alike."

That one summary heading is followed by another heading: "And lastly the need for the remedial legislative action based on the Allis-Chalmers actual

---

[14]Harry A. Millis and Emily Clark Brown, *From the Wagner Act to Taft-Hartley* (Chicago: University of Chicago Press, 1950), p. 171. Cf. U.S. Congress, Senate, 86th Cong., 2d sess., Report No. 1189, Part 2, *Final Report* of the Select Committee on Improper Activities in the Labor or Management Field Pursuant to S. Res. 44 and 249, March 15, 1960, pp. 305ff., 141, 158. For denial of membership and equal protection under the Wagner Act, see N. W. Chamberlain, "Union Obligations Under the National Labor Relations Act," *American Economic Review*, 37 (March 1947): 170ff.

[15]Hartley, *Our New Labor Policy.* Cf. Robinson, *Meany*, p. 145; Richter, *Political Purpose*, pp. 150ff.

experience."[16] In sum, this company's plea was not based on complaints about the existing labor law or the existing contract. If one ignores the political language about the strike and the picketing (termed "illegal"), the sole basis for the argument favoring labor-law revision was the alleged excessive power of the local at the workplace and, paradoxically, its violation of rank-and-file members' rights.

In his introductory remarks, Story perhaps unintentionally revealed how little specific or real complaint his firm had with the administrative fairness of the existing labor law. Here he unconsciously revealed how much reliance his firm was now placing on the "menace of communistic union leadership" to bring about its long-sought change in plant relations. "I will lead off Section 1," he argued, "by laying the foundation for our presentation, namely the menace of communism in the labor movement and more particularly the menace of communistic union leadership."[17]

Lest the committee be complacent about the dangers to the United States, Story also referred menacingly to communism in the Soviet Union and in France. Possibly because of the absence of strikes in the USSR, the brief found it unnecessary to specify details about that communist system. However, Allis-Chalmers dwelled on evidence of "communistic" strikes in France. Without bothering to justify the presumed connection of the French unrest with the Milwaukee dispute or the U.S. labor law, or to explain the economic factors that might have led the CP-led CGT in France to call its strikes, the company witness said that changes in American law were needed "to make certain [the] experience of France with communistic control of labor can't happen here." (The phrase echoed language used in a contemporary novel by Sinclair Lewis.) Perhaps to make sure the committee did not become too distracted to miss the company's point, the brief also linked Allis-Chalmers' opposition to Local 248 with the more traditional anti-union theory being advanced by the NAM and its subsidiary organizations: "Thus, the communist plan is to destroy capitalism by undermining management's control of its business."[18]

Story's formulations and Allis-Chalmers' plans eventually had their effect. While the conference bill as passed by both houses over President Truman's veto was the result of many compromises, it incorporated several of Allis-Chalmers' recommendations, including, notably, Section 9(h). This

[16]Points Nine and Ten, Allis-Chalmers brief, p. 24.
[17]Allis-Chalmers brief, introductory remarks, pp. 1–8.
[18]Ibid. Cf. Howell John Harris, *The Right to Manage: Industrial Relations Policies of American Business* (Madison: University of Wisconsin Press, 1982).

noncommunist-affidavit provision barred from using the new labor law or the reconstructed National Labor Relations Board (NLRB), not only those unions that had offices who were Communist Party members but also, more loosely, those who advocated "overthrow of the United States Government by force or by any illegal or unconstitutional methods." Some employers used noncompliance by a union (that is, failure to sign the Section 9(h) affidavits) as sufficient reason to withdraw from a contract and, in some cases, to discharge union militants. (In the case of Allis-Chalmers, most of the disciplining was done, after Taft-Hartley went into effect, by the international. This is discussed in Chapter 5.)

Story's presentation of Local 248 history and its 1946 "political" stoppage of course influenced the tone and substance of ensuing questions put to the UAW witnesses who followed the company's representatives. The atmosphere was distinctly less friendly and less respectful. When union members tried, unsuccessfully, to give their versions of the Allis-Chalmers strike and related labor matters, they were met with new rigidity and hostility. Although the 1946–7 strike was the focus of the Auto Workers' evidence, and was therefore a direct response to the company's testimony, the committee was quite evidently ready to punish labor, and radical labor in particular.

Chairman Hartley and his colleagues showed by their questioning of R. J. Thomas and local Allis-Chalmers union witnesses that the committee had decided to politicize that stoppage to help the committee strategists advance Section 9(h) and the conference bill as a whole. Even Democratic members of the committee, including not only the Dixiecrats but the liberal Democrat John F. Kennedy, concurred with this politicization of the dispute. This concurrence essentially rested on the GOP members' desire for labor change and the liberals' desire to dissociate themselves from, and to curb, labor radicalism.

How could such a turnaround occur? After all, this committee and its staff knew the Wagner Act history: that it had been successful in achieving its purpose of encouraging collective bargaining. It should have known about the authoritative Bureau of Labor Statistics analysis of the 1946 strikes; that analysis, which included the Allis-Chalmers stoppages at West Allis and elsewhere, revealed a standard form of economic causation.

The answer lies mainly in nonunion politics. Kennedy and other liberal Democratic members were knowledgeable enough about labor relations to know that strikes or stoppages were commonplace in the course of normal collective bargaining, whatever the party affiliation of union officers. The committee members as a whole, with the possible exception of the highly idiosyncratic Clare Hoffman (R., Mich.), were rational men. It is hard to credit that they believed eight or nine thousand men and women in a huge industrial plant would walk off their jobs and stay out for about a year all through the manipulation of a handful of "communists."

Again, one must consider the political atmosphere of the moment to explain why such an implausible interpretation was effective even among well-informed, pro-union liberals. By 1947, Congress' and the president's fears about communism abroad had brought about the passage of the National Security Act of 1947, under which Truman established the Central Intelligence Agency. His own "loyalty" executive order was issued during the very first months of Taft-Hartley. Some Democratic and Republican members of Congress were now more open in their "nigger"-baiting and Jew-baiting as well as labor- and Red-baiting. Not only the administration and Congress but commentators in the daily press and radio; many churches; all major employers' associations; and even some central labor bodies were showing panic and helping to create panic reminiscent of the Palmer Raid days after World War I. In the atmosphere of the day, strikes tended to be quickly associated with crises abroad. This spilled over into fear of domestic strikes and in many cases genuine alarm about the minuscule Communist Party element in the CIO. Some liberals and other reform-minded individuals saw this trend as purulence needing detoxification. But prominent people in Congress, and even some key labor leaders, felt called upon to declare themselves against the "menace." Whatever the cause, Congress was responding to international communism as the danger – a danger transcending both impartiality and legal safeguards. For Hartley's committee, the prolonged Local 248 stoppage and its well-known left-wing leadership proved to be a godsend.

For this key congressional committee, it was now immaterial that the international executive board of the Auto Workers had routinely sanctioned the Local 248 stoppage as merely one of many labor-management conflicts in mid 1946. At that time of militancy in the UAW, factional voices were muted, and commentators generally had not yet sensed the potentials of that old factional split for a counterattack against labor. In 1947, however, an intensified level of factionalism had erupted in the pivotal UAW, coinciding with a new thrust against the left in the CIO. Vice-President Reuther had become President Reuther on a right-wing platform. While he would soon make extended contract gains for the Auto Workers, he had won support from the media for a purging of the left within the UAW and the CIO. At the UAW, the old factional battle raged at a new level of intensity as the "mechanical majority" of the board stopped him from taking full control on behalf of the right-wing coalition that had elected him president. Although Reuther was demanding my neck and the dismissal of other center-left staffers (see the Postlude), the left-center coalition was still relatively intact in the UAW in the spring of 1947, as it was in the CIO as a whole. But that coalition was very precarious. In this context, the committee and the star corporate witness, the Allis-Chalmers Company, were not being extremist but merely joining a larger grouping forming inside the CIO and outside as well, all intent on isolating the left, including Local 248.

Under different circumstances, such a labor witness as R.J. Thomas, known in the CIO and in Congress as a moderate and a close associate of CIO president Murray, with a rank-and-file background, would have been seized upon as an important witness for a labor-law hearing. However, he was now brushed off as merely another agitator. Phil Murray, the committee knew, had refused to personally express his interest in the strike. This was not a denial of the value of and the necessity for the strike weapon. It was, however, a political statement: Murray, the CIO boss, was thereby signaling to his own membership and others that the CIO henceforth would be moving to the right.

To my knowledge, Murray himself did not appear as a witness, nor did he ask to appear at these crucially important hearings. He sent one of his most conservative aides, Van Bittner, to give the CIO's testimony. Had Murray appeared, he might have given similar traditional CIO interpretations of the law, of collective bargaining, and of condemnation of communism. However, he probably would have felt called upon to back the strike itself. But in these months of 1947, he was actively engaged in terminating the left-center coalitions that were in control of many CIO councils, including the Industrial Union Council of Milwaukee County and the State of Wisconsin CIO, where Local 248 was an active and important influence. Murray had energized his own Steel Workers to intervene on behalf of a right-wing slate, even to the extent of removing Meyer Adelman from the Steel Workers' staff because Adelman had been supportive of the local, its strike, and its role in Milwaukee and Wisconsin politics.

The Wisconsin state CIO convention of 1946, like the CIO national executive board, had voted to back the Allis-Chalmers strike. For this state CIO support, however, there was a quid pro quo that reflected a general shift in politics as well as the CIO "pro-communist" centrists' own wavering about the remaining power of the left. A *New York Times* correspondent noted that R. J. Thomas agreed to have Robert Buse, then president of the Allis-Chalmers local, withdraw from the presidency of the state council. In the event, Buse and also M. L. Heinritz, who had long held the position of secretary-treasurer of the Wisconsin Industrial Union Council and was, like Buse, prominently identified with both left-center politics and with the Local 248 strike, were defeated by right-wingers. Clearly Thomas was not moving to the left of Phil Murray. And Local 248 president Buse was staying with Thomas on this issue of Wisconsin labor politics. Under a headline "Leftist Rule Ends in Wisconsin CIO," the *Times* reporter described the emergence of the right: "The right wing broke today the domination which the left wing had exercised over the State CIO since it was founded nine years ago." Pointing to the motion of a Milwaukee UE delegate – the UE was a pillar on the left locally as it was nationally – to support the Allis-Chalmers workers by a wider work holiday, the *Times* again focused on a new moderation and accommodation at the center: "R. J. Thomas' caution to delegates was that a work holiday was 'not a matter on which the Council could decide'; that the international unions 'had supreme authority' on such a question. Robert Buse, then in the Chair, ruled the UE motion out of order."[19]

All this collaboration with the right by Buse and Thomas was ignored when these two, joined by the founding president of Local 248, Harold Christoffel, appeared before the new labor committee a few months later. The committee treated all three with contempt, as irresponsible and subversive. The committee planners, continuing their basic strategy of frightening the country about communists, showed no more interest in the subtleties of union factionalism than they did in the union's substantive evidence on the 1946–7 strike or the proposed law. Instead, member after member, leaning on the Story–Allis-Chalmers brief, pressed each union witness to answer political questions about the theory and practice of communism at home and abroad.

Union Testimony

When R. J. Thomas volunteered to go to Washington to testify, he was confident he would be the star labor witness. He regarded himself as the first of two international union vice-presidents and a world-famous labor leader. He could boast of his friendship with Philip Murray. He was also the closest counterpart to the chief company witness, Harold Story.

The committee strategists, however, had their own plan for labor witnesses. Their agenda called for a star appearance by Christoffel, recently returned from the U.S. Army and now honorary president of Local 248. "Chris" was on the strike committee but was no longer an elected officer (although the title

[19]*New York Times*, December 16, 1946.

of honorary president reflected the place he occupied in the local's pantheon of heroes). But the committee insisted on his being given top-priority billing, superseding international vice-president Thomas.

Rapping his gavel with more than the customary tap, Chairman Hartley opened the proceedings on March 12, 1947, by calling for Christoffel. There was no response. Looking around the room, he rapped again and called for order. He called out for "Mr. Robert Buse." At that point, Thomas walked up to the dais. He told Hartley, "I happen to be R. J. Thomas, Vice-President of the international union, who is in charge of the Allis-Chalmers strike and if arrangements could be made, I would like to go on first."[20]

Instead of complying with Thomas' rather pontifical request to testify first, as would have been done routinely by most committees, Chairman Hartley took the unusual position that the local union people must appear first. Thomas then ordered me to fetch Christoffel and Buse. Hartley actually stopped the proceedings and announced, "The committee will suspend until they arrive."[21]

The UAW side sensed a congressional plot: that the primary objective of the committee chairman at this point was to get Christoffel and Buse to the stand not for their expertise or prestige, not for any perceptible legislative purpose, but solely because they were presumed to be vulnerable on the communist question. This was not as foolish as it might sound. The strategy conformed to the underlying purpose of the House committee: to shift union attention away from the substantive charges and toward the sponsors' "noncommunist" preferences, and to frighten Congress and the public over the "menace."

The union-toughened R. J. Thomas persisted. In a formal sense at least, he did win the opening position for the UAW-CIO testimony. The proceedings show nevertheless that the committee's agenda prevailed. Christoffel, not Thomas or Buse, became the star witness as well as the star defendant in a committee-inspired indictment for perjury.

Thomas' direct testimony and expertise, as well as the elaborate UAW brief

[20]U.S. Congress, House, 80th Cong., 1st sess., Committee on Education and Labor, *Amendments to the National Labor Relations Act*, vol. 3, pp. 1973ff. Thomas could have been examined for his shop experience as well as his national and international expertise. He had had a Horatio Alger–type rise in the auto union, having been a welder and honest-to-goodness rank-and-file type when selected as a compromise candidate to fill the vacancy left when Homer Martin was ousted from the UAW-CIO presidency in 1938–9. As a semiskilled worker from the assembly lines of Chrysler Corporation, where he had once served as a company union officer before affiliating with the CIO and joining in the recognition strikes, he might have illuminated the rise of the CIO from a shop perspective and shed light on the strike weapon for organizing and for bargaining.

[21]Ibid., p. 2049.

dealing with the stoppage and the historic labor-relations pattern at Allis-Chalmers, were largely ignored by Hartley and his committee. Thomas had time to introduce himself and to recite his wartime and postwar public positions: member of the National War Labor Board and CIO delegate at the president's Labor-Management Conference in 1945. He then tried, valiantly but futilely, to interest the members of the committee in his views on both the Allis-Chalmers strike and the pending labor legislation. Except for Detroit congressman John Lesinski, none of the committee members present showed interest. Lesinski and other members did push Thomas, however, to give his views of the theory and practice of communism. He had anticipated such questions, and declared:

I am not a communist, a socialist, a Trotskyite or any other brand of radical. I have never been, neither do I expect to be, for I am, first and last, an American worker who believes in the trade union movement, and by choice a member of the UAW-CIO.[22]

Although Thomas was highly credentialed and was in charge of the Local 248 strike for the international union, Chairman Hartley cut him off before he could go into the substance of the proposed law or the strike. Hartley and his strategy-minded staffers, including Irving R. McCann of Allis-Chalmers and other corporate lawyer volunteers, clearly preferred to crowd out legitimate testimony and dwell on one narrow field of politics. For this purpose, they wished to see Thomas disappear. They had obviously decided to focus on Christoffel and Buse. "Mr. Thomas," Hartley said in dismissing him, "I have no desire to limit your testimony unnecessarily, that [sic] as you know, this day was set aside to hear Mr. Buse and Mr. Christoffel."

Under established legislative custom, Thomas would have had no trouble being heard at length and without rancor. He now sought a normal industrial-relations solution to the Allis-Chalmers strike; moreover, his own union background was moderate and apolitical. But there was a more crucial internal labor union consideration for Hartley et al., namely, that Thomas now symbolized the hated left-center CIO coalition. Thomas was treasurer of the CIO Political Action Committee. This was a political aspect of the CIO unionism that was anathema to many and that clearly had relevance for labor-law consideration. The Taft-Hartley bill did seek to curb labor politics; but in this respect as well Thomas was ignored by the committee. The unrecorded fact was that Hartley's committee, like the various "un-American" committees in Congress, the FBI, and other executive agencies of the federal government in 1946–7, was in the grip of the same illiberal dynamic. All, in varying de-

[22]Ibid., pp. 2057ff.

grees, wanted to see the end of political activity by unions. There was no taste now for the type of macrosocietal change that the CIO, backing the New Deal, had waged since 1936–7. Thomas, although anticommunist, had been for several years a supporter of the left-center coalition in the UAW-CIO and in the CIO PAC.

Thomas, a direct participant in pro-union government labor-relations programs – during the Second World War as a labor member of the National War Labor Board, and in November-December 1945 as a CIO delegate to the president's Labor-Management Conference – was now as suspect in governmental circles as he was in the new Congress. We have previously seen Truman's impatient housing-strike memo while Thomas was still UAW president. Along with that display of extreme irritation, the president was about to issue his 1947 executive order declaring that a "loyalty" campaign would be launched within the federal service. His own Department of Justice would enforce that order. The major bureau in Justice, the FBI, was continuing to intervene in the UAW's factional politics, essentially for the purpose of ousting the left and those centrists willing to accept the left. Thus, a 1947 memo written by E. M. Ladd, special agent in charge of the Detroit office, to John Edgar Hoover clearly shows the FBI pursuing such a distinctly factional role within the pivotal UAW and so indirectly supporting the politically motivated actions of the Republican-dominated Education and Labor Committee. Agent Ladd, too, perceived the Local 248 dispute as a determining factor in the drive to oust Reds and centrist non-Reds such as R. J. Thomas. "At the present time," Ladd wrote, "Thomas is charged with the direction of the Allis-Chalmers strike. All officials of the Allis-Chalmers Local number 248 are known to be Communist Party members or very sympathetic to the Communist cause."[23]

---

[23]U.S. Department of Justice, Federal Bureau of Investigation, Freedom of Information Act report obtained by Irving Richter, containing copy of memorandum by Ladd to J. Edgar Hoover, March 8, 1947. The FBI's long faction-oriented watch of Local 248 and associated CIO and CP Wisconsin leaders is further shown in the following excerpt from a heavily censored report on the Second International Education Conference, UAW-CIO, held at the Pfister Hotel in Milwaukee in January 1945. "It should be noted that NED SPARKS [a CP functionary], MEL HEINRITZ [left-wing CIO state secretary-treasurer] and HAROLD CHRISTOFFEL were at the Pfister Hotel on 1-6-45, and were observed on the seventh floor of that hotel, where the conference was held. It should be noted also that the seventh floor was devoted entirely to this conference. In addition to these individuals being present, it should also be noted that ESTHER HANDLER was listed as a member of the Arrangement Committee of the Conference." In the copy I received, the balance of the page is blacked out except for a heading that reads "Influence of the CPA [Communist Political Association – wartime change made by the Communist Party] in the Conference." By 1947, "CPA" had been dropped and "Party" reinstituted.

The Communist Party of Wisconsin made no secret of its role in the CIO, UAW Local 248,

Possibly because labor itself was so divided, it received little support from liberals on the committee. After Thomas' brush-off as a witness, I suggested to him that I meet with Representative John F. Kennedy. R. J. responded that he and the local officials were harassed by Kennedy as well as by other committee members, as indeed they were. But I urged that Kennedy was less unfriendly than the Republicans. (There were on the committee three more liberal and New Dealish Democratic members: Augustine ("Gus") Kelley of Pennsylvania and the New Yorkers Arthur C. Klein and Adam Clayton Powell. But they were absent during meetings on the Allis-Chalmers situation.)

Kennedy, whatever his subsequent metamorphoses, did not fit conventional typologies. He favored unionism and even industrial unionism of the CIO variety. He dissented from some of the findings of the GOP majority. But he was also intent on ending pro-communist influence in unions by ousting the left and those centrists supporting the left. In 1947, this was of high and imminent importance to Kennedy's political future. It could win votes not only from labor but also from Democratic leaders, especially southern Democrats who couldn't abide unions. Whatever his motivations – whether pragmatic or ideological or both – Kennedy had cited to witness Buse (from evidence in the company brief) a range of what he considered pro-communist activities at Local 248, from circulation of a 1938 petition to free Communist Party general secretary Earl Browder from prison, to circulating nominating petitions for the communist candidate for governor, Eisenscher, *and* for a Democratic candidate named Boborowicz. The latter, Kennedy said, though a Democrat had been "exposed as a pro-communist."[24]

---

and the local's 1946 strikes. Sigmund Eisenscher, a former 248 member, told a Wisconsin State Historical Society interviewer a few years ago (and repeated to this writer in 1988) that he never made a secret of his own membership in the Communist Party while "legally" running for governor of Wisconsin as an independent in 1946. What led to the company's prominent reference to his nominating petition, he told me in 1988, was Allis-Chalmers' "fury" at his success in getting some 800 of his 5,000 required signatures from among the pickets during the strike. Prior to incorporating all these signatures in the above-mentioned Taft-Hartley brief, the firm had placed display ads in the two Milwaukee dailies and had then "with no sense of shame" mailed all the names of the signers, a "sure blacklist," he told me (phone interview, June 25, 1988).

[24]Hearings, pp. 2011, 2013–14. In "On the Road to Camelot," *Labor History*, 2, no. 2 (Spring 1980): 280–90, based on the transcript of Kennedy's abusive questioning of Buse, S. Diamond of Columbia University provides some history of the strike and of Buse's role in the shop and local. Diamond had been a UAW research assistant in Detroit, doing much of the publicity for the stoppage, for the international union brief, and for the left-center UAW caucus. He had major responsibility for the main caucus publication against Reuther, a pamphlet entitled "The Boss' Boy." For the same issue of *Labor History*, I wrote a much shorter piece dealing with Representative Richard M. Nixon's questions to Buse and Buse's answers. My article stresses the inherent back-to-work problem associated with any long strike, and how Nixon tried "to turn this familiar problem into a political [communist] conspiracy" in the case of Local 248

"Congressman," I said to the handsome freshman from Massachusetts in his office, "do you know the industrial relations history of this company?" He said no, and seemed interested in hearing what I had to say. He listened thoughtfully as I explained the historic Allis-Chalmers policy of opposing all independent unions and all forms of genuine collective bargaining. I then described the local and international union attempts first to avoid the 1946–7 stoppage and then to end it by arbitration and later by fact finding.

In response, Representative Kennedy expressed to me his own impatience with anti-unionism. But he also made clear that he was against communism and the communist-centrist ties in the CIO and in the UAW-CIO. Kennedy was very thoughtful and careful with his words. I recall his saying he regarded R. J. Thomas as pro-communist and Walter Reuther as an "intelligent but nonpolitical trade union leader." I tried to talk about the stoppage. He replied only indirectly. Instead of addressing the 1946–7 strike, he spoke about the more controversial 1941 stoppage. "That was a commie strike," he said. "It hurt the unions everywhere." When I brought up the question of Buse's and Christoffel's possible perjury citations at the hearing, Kennedy said he would have to go along with whatever the committee decided. (I will return to this discussion in Chapter 5.)

While labor found Republicans and Democrats solidly aligned behind an anticommunist front, interested in neither the substance of labor nor the causes of strikes, many unionists were also aware that their own strongest leaders were not lending support to the "stop Taft-Hartley" propaganda rhetoric. UAW-CIO president Walter Reuther would have been a strong witness against Taft-Hartley. As already indicated, he was a favorite of the media, which frequently cited his election in 1946 as a symbol of the decline of Communist Party influence in labor, an important blow to the left-center coalition in the CIO, and a sign of right-wing resurgence. But he had not been invited to testify and, to my knowledge, had not sought an invitation to the vital House committee hearings. I had written about his appearance and the opposition he expressed to "anti-labor" bills before the Senate committee.[25] I

(pp. 277–8). Reproductions of the company brief very prominently featured the above-named nominating petitions.

[25]Richter, "Dirty Work Behind Closed Doors," *Minnesota Labor,* April 4, 1947. A Federated Press (perceived as left wing, and managed by a noncommunist left-wing anarchist type, Carl Haessler) release in early 1947 noted that Reuther was Red-baited by GOP Senators Ball and Taft, who called him a socialist – denied by Reuther – apparently because of Reuther's leadership role in the J. I. Case strike (authorized by the international and settled in 1946) (*Headlight* [organ of UAW Buick Local 599], March 4, 1947). This strike authorized at the same time as the Local 248 stoppage, was relatively free of factional controversy and did not figure in the House hearings.

ignored the fact that Reuther, convinced that Local 248 had been created and was directed by the Communist Party, was at best lukewarm about the Allis-Chalmers strike. He was also convinced that removal of alleged communist staffers – as he told the UAW international executive board at Louisville in 1947 during the "Richter case" (see Postlude) – was the best way for CIO unions to survive the postwar "witch hunt."

Had the more important House labor committee wished to pursue the subject of "political" strikes and the related question of communist influence, the UAW's president might have been a valuable witness. He was the only international officer who had worked in a Soviet factory; he had a rich background in labor and radicalism; and he had been international vice-president of the UAW-CIO and director of its General Motors Department. He had won a new contract for General Motors workers after leading the first great postwar strike. During the General Motors strike, Reuther initiated the highly political demand for a "look at the books," in support of which he orchestrated a series of supporting statements by political and community leaders. That stoppage was settled on the basis of a government formula. In short, this strike had been in a real sense political.

Moreover, Reuther had shown he was a man of ideas, with much political savvy. He was also known as a friend of many in Congress, including Jack Kennedy. He had established a reputation as an expert on production problems associated with war planning, was a skilled negotiator and strike leader, and was in 1947 known not only in Washington but worldwide as president of the nation's largest union.[26]

However, had he appeared before the House Committee on Education and Labor, it might have upset committee strategists and such friends as Kennedy. Reuther would have been pressed not only to dissociate himself from communism, as Thomas had, but to identify the 1946–7 and 1941 Local 248 strikes as communist-inspired. The astute Reuther was known to take precisely that view of both stoppages. But he was not about to go public with such a statement on either stoppage before the notoriously anti-union House committee in 1947. In union circles, this could have amounted to treason. But he did go on record in the national leadership meetings of the UAW-CIO on the 1946–7 strike and Local 248 (see Chapter 5).

The union's side was struck a harsh blow when the Hartley Committee in early June 1947 forwarded a perjury citation of Christoffel via the full House,

[26]For an insightful view of Reuther's role in the UAW and CIO, and the political implications of the stoppage, see David Brody, *Workers in Industrial America: Essays on the 20th Century Struggle* (New York: Oxford University Press, 1980), pp. 45–6, 189, 192–4, 175–7.

later supported by a federal grand jury. My syndicated column of June 19, 1947, regularly carried by the Local 248 special edition of the State of Wisconsin *CIO News,* reported on the case. Reissued as a leaflet by the union's Allis-Chalmers strike committee, this account summarized the committee's punitive action, described my interview with Kennedy, and clearly defended the local leadership. The beleaguered local gave my story a banner headline of its own, reading "Giant Labor Frameup Plotted by House Labor Group." My account, as well as the leaflet, featured "irregularities in House procedures" in the citation of Christoffel and my Kennedy interview. This story charged bias by the subcommittee (of which Kennedy was a member) appointed by Hartley sent to Milwaukee to investigate ex-president Christoffel, and referred to Kennedy's role in pressing for the federal indictment of Christoffel.

The strike committee put a subheading, "Loaded Probe," over my description of the irregular congressional procedure that was later cited by the U.S. Supreme Court in overturning the indictment:

The evidence on which the Grand Jury is now proceeding was compiled by a three-man subcommittee sent by Rep. Hartley to Milwaukee – Rep. Charles Kersten (R., Wis.), Rep. Thomas L. Owens (R., Ill.) and Rep. John Kennedy (D., Mass.). Each of them showed extreme hostility to Buse and Christoffel at the public hearing in Washington before they were picked by Hartley to go to Milwaukee . . .

Despite his smooth Hollywood-type prosecutor's manner, the Subcommittee Chairman, Charles Kersten, betrayed the most bitter hatred for both Christoffel and Buse during the Washington hearing. Company officials campaigned for his election, and closely guided his work on the Labor Committee. Earlier he told Buse: "You fellows might be right, but I'm on the other side." When Buse denied Communist Party membership, Kersten replied: "My yardstick on Communist Party membership is simple: if a man criticizes the Franco government, he's a commie."[27]

The strike committee then reported to its readers, the strikers and those who had gone back to work, Kennedy's unusually candid response to my questions about the frame-up of Christoffel by the subcommittee and grand jury:

I asked the third member of the subcommittee, the handsome, boyish-looking John Kennedy, son of the former Ambassador to Great Britain, why a perjury charge was being pushed against labor witnesses only, while the company wasn't being bothered. Kennedy told me: "The 1941 Allis-Chalmers strike was a commie strike. It hurt the government. It hurt the union. So we've got to use any technicality we can, just like the government did when it got Al Capone on an income tax evasion."[28]

---

[27]Local 248, UAW-CIO, strike leaflet, undated [1947]. In its later dismissal of the case against Christoffel, the U.S. Supreme Court cited the absence of a committee quorum when the action by the committee was initiated without going into any constitutional questions.
[28]Ibid.

As the leaflet suggests, the local recognized but found it expedient to do nothing more than indirectly publicize the fact that the strike had become embroiled in UAW factional politics. Like the FBI, the Education and Labor Committee gave no serious consideration to this industrial dispute, but turned the strike into a political football. Although the leaders could hardly concede the point, their strike became a significant factor in passage of Taft-Hartley. Later it became a factor in the ongoing factional struggle for control of the UAW-CIO.

The "political activities" of the local received considerable attention at the time from observers of internal labor politics, notably writers Howe and Widick, and later from Bert Cochran. With full access to key participants at the international headquarters of the UAW-CIO, Howe and Widick concluded in an influential book that the strike was a "fiasco" because it was "contaminated by damaging political activities." This was written immediately after the company made a similar charge, during the height of the CIO expulsion trials of "Communist-dominated" affiliates and after the placing of an administrator over the local by the UAW international executive board. With unintended irony, Howe and Widick noted the central role played by factionalism in both the final stages of the strike and in passage of the new labor law. What they termed the fiasco at West Allis and "damaging political activities" helped eliminate the left and center from the UAW-CIO and thereby helped consolidate Walter Reuther's leadership.[29]

Whatever their own preferences, Howe and Widick explicitly recognized that international union politics, featured by Allis-Chalmers management and the Hartley Committee, played a significant role in the conduct and termination of this stoppage and also in the passage of Taft-Hartley. One may reasonably infer that the authors agreed with the basic premise of the sponsors of the new labor law, namely, that this local union and its 1946–7 strike were political.

Cochran in 1977 approached the subject from an anticommunist but more union-informed viewpoint. His "Showdown in Auto and Electrical Unions," flavored by a Trotskyist perspective, comes down hard on the CPUSA. He gives valuable insights on the Communist Party leadership in auto and electrical manufacturing and on the factional splits in both unions. He shows that Local 248 resolutions, while reflecting CPUSA views, were decidedly non-

---

[29]Irving Howe and B. J. Widick, *The UAW and Walter Reuther* (New York: Random House, 1949), pp. 165–70. The IEB minutes discussed in Chapter 5 below are designed to shed additional light on the international union's policies during the period of the Allis-Chalmers stoppage before and after Taft-Hartley.

revolutionary. Unlike Howe and Widick, however, Cochran emphasizes management's objective: the historical opposition by the Allis-Chalmers Company both to AFL unions and, especially, to Local 248.

Cochran does not evade the UAW factional differences and the aggravation of those splits by Taft-Hartley. He describes in vivid prose the "disintegration" of the "Addes-[Thomas]" caucus following enactment of Taft-Hartley and the defeat of the strike. He also shows the significant effect of that internal UAW shift on the political shift of the CIO under Murray.[30] Cochran's central point, however, is that management cared very little about the political coloration of union leaders chosen by workers. What was objectionable to the company was the effective collective bargaining system inaugurated by Local 248 and based on a dense system of elected shop stewards. This local believed not only in collective bargaining but in widening workers' claims of control over the shop floor and in creating a political role for unions locally and nationally. It was in response to the local's shop-floor militancy that the company took the bold step of destroying the grievance machinery by unilateral action in 1946 before taking political action in 1947. The company was well aware of this union's severe factionalism. Its primary goal was, however, total destruction of the local's independent power.

Until 1947, Local 248 was a standard independent industrial union. The political affiliations of its officers and the resolutions it passed were subordinate to that fact. Company managers at Allis-Chalmers had been forced to reluctantly share power with it even before the Wagner Act and Wisconsin's "Little Wagner Act." The state act was weakened before the war. But the New Deal labor law had survived the first onslaught against it in the prewar period as well as during the war. It was still the basic labor law in 1947.

While the National Association of Manufacturers and its member firms, including even Allis-Chalmers, had become reconciled to government-encouraged collective bargaining, they all wanted as a first basic step toward restoring management's power for the postwar period to reverse the Wagner Act and eliminate militant rank-and-file unionism from the workplace, and to end independent-minded labor politics.

Despite its compromises, Taft-Hartley was a strong beginning for organized

[30]Bert Cochran, *Labor and Communism: The Conflict That Shaped American Unions* (Princeton, N.J.: Princeton University Press, 1977), ch. 2. Cf. Ronald W. Schatz, *The Electrical Workers: A History of Labor at General Electric and Westinghouse* (Champaign: University of Illinois Press, 1983); Harvey A. Levenstein, *Communism, Anticommunism and the CIO* (Westport, Conn.: Greenwood, 1981), pp. 217ff., 199, 234ff.; Jeremy Brecher, *Strike! The True History of Mass Insurgence in America from 1877 to the Present* . . . (San Francisco: Straight Arrow, 1973); Jack Barbash, "The Politics of American Labor," *Challenge*, May–June 1976, p. 32.

employers. As Representative Donald L. O'Toole put it – rather too strongly – during House debate, "The bill [as adopted by the conferees] was written sentence by sentence, paragraph by paragraph, page by page by the National Association of Manufacturers."[31] With more authority, Senator Taft said, "The bill . . . covers about three-quarters of the matters pressed upon us very strenuously by the employers."[32] Senator Taft and Representative Hartley both stated, as previously noted here, that they were interested in curbing the power of labor leaders and unions while providing what they viewed as a bill of rights for workers.

There were indeed abuses of worker rights within organized labor. In this change of labor law, however, Congress actually strengthened the hand of national union leaders, giving no significant concessions to the needs of workers, organized or unorganized. By enactment of the new law, the 80th Congress maintained a framework of collective bargaining but added a new, highly complex structure of government intervention in labor relations. Exploiting the general fear of prosecution under various sections of the act, and especially by implementation of Section 9(h), the new National Labor Relations Board (aided by many important union leaders of the day) undermined the electoral rights of the rank and file by denying them the right to elect officers of their own choosing. Once they decided to conform to the new law, including the affidavit requirements of the reconstructed National Labor Relations Board, the unions subjected themselves to new employer offensives, to greater government regulation, and to tighter national leadership. The requirement to report annually on the political coloration of elected officers at local and higher levels of the union movement was one-sided and was eventually declared unconstitutional. But even the strongly voluntarist American Federation of Labor rushed to comply with the affidavit requirement.

Thanks to favorable market conditions, most unions were able to maintain aggregate growth for a few years. Material gains were made under collective bargaining, some gains clearly going beyond traditional bread-and-butter issues. But the scope and effectiveness of bargaining were limited by the new law. As market conditions improved, and as the Cold War political climate persisted, the once-militant CIO expelled its left wing in an effort to show a new image. Employers often found it possible to defeat union organizing and to regain for industry much of the ground lost during the New Deal and the Second World War years.

[31]Press release from O'Toole's office. Interestingly, that press release was drafted by me.
[32]Quoted by Fagan Ginger and Christiano, *The Cold War Against Labor*, p. 243. Cf. Brody, *Workers in Industrial America*, pp. 178–82.

While enhancing power at the top, the new law aggravated old labor splits and created new divisions. The house of labor, already weakened by old splits, was further fragmented by Taft-Hartley. The united front of business and industry was sustained and strengthened.

5

THE AFTERMATH OF TAFT-HARTLEY:
REAL BEHAVIOR VERSUS
UNION RHETORIC

This chapter deals mainly with de facto union behavior in the immediate aftermath of the Labor-Management Relations Act of 1947, a turning point in U.S. labor history. One can approach this period of labor change from a variety of perspectives: cultural, economic, political, social. For the present analysis of labor's behavior, I have chosen to focus on the unions' political action. Since a portrayal of political behavior requires at least some consideration of other societal features, I will be referring to a variety of nonpolitical, nonlabor phenomena that I think contributed to labor's political responses.

The Veto Message

I begin with the veto message of the president of the United States – a decidedly political event cited as important by both the American Federation of Labor and the Congress of Industrial Organizations in their support of Truman in 1948. Both decided to campaign for Harry Truman's reelection largely on the basis of that veto.

President Truman's controversial veto of the new legislation, which both houses voted to override, appears to have been a straightforward pro-labor analysis of H.R. 3020, the final conference bill. The ten-page message shows Truman's labor expertise and covers the major legislative features of interest to the AFL and CIO. It exhibits a rare frankness about congressional and other fears. And it reflects the ambivalence and contradictions in the Truman administration. Truman directly addressed what he regarded as the central political danger confronting the country in 1947: communism. He expressed agreement with the "objective" of Congress as well as the anger some labor union leaders felt about the unfairness of the entire reporting section. Addressing the requirement of reporting noncommunist affidavits, Section 9(h), he first expresses his agreement with that objective; he then asserts his opposition to this "burdensome" reporting requirement. "Congress," he declared, "intended to assist labor organizations to rid themselves of Communist officers. With this I am in full accord." He did not mention his own loyalty order of 1947 that was then being enforced by his attorney general. That order was helping create the very same "great fear" cited before as a central characteristic of the immediate postwar period. The 80th Congress capitalized on this fear in devising Section 9(h). The Republicans had used essentially the same fear in winning their 1946 victory at the polls with the Communism, Confusion, Chaos campaign, and earlier House committees had used it. Now, while Truman agreed that Section 9(h) was an ideological objective he shared with Congress, he also feared that this part of the bill would result in more strikes:

The mere refusal by a single individual to sign the required affidavit would prevent an entire national labor union from being certified for purposes of collective bargaining. Such a union would have to win all its objectives by strike, rather than by orderly procedure under the law. The union and the affected industry would be disrupted for perhaps a long period of time while violent electioneering, charges and countercharges split open the union ranks. The only result of this provision would be confusion and disorder, which is exactly what the Communists desire.[1]

"This provision in the bill," he concluded, "is an attempt to solve difficult problems of industrial democracy by recourse to oversimplified legal devices. I consider that this provision would increase, rather than decrease, disruptive effects of Communists in our labor movement."[2]

Most of the unions' leaders would soon be signing the affidavits and complying with Taft-Hartley at the very time they were rallying behind Truman's candidacy. They also, in many cases, began raiding noncomplying, "communist-dominated" CIO affiliates and, in some cases, going to the FBI and other investigative bodies. Many union leaders were already high-profile figures, but they could be assured of receiving new favorable publicity by exposing "communists" and fellow travelers remaining in leadership positions in their unions.[3]

---

[1]U.S. Congress, House, *Message from the President of the United States: Returning Without His Approval the Bill H.R. 3020 Entitled the "Labor-Management Relations Act, 1947,"* 80th Cong., 1st sess., 1947, p. 10.

[2]Ibid., pp. 9–10. This was a reference to the national CIO and those of its left-wing unions that had announced they were going to resist the act. See n. 3.

[3]Contrary to Truman's expectation, most of the unions influenced by the Communist Party, after declaring they would resist the act, decided that it was in their institutional interest to sign the affidavits required under Section 9(h).

A few of the disparate acts by CP-influenced unions are suggested later in this chapter. My examples are not meant to be a complete sampling of reactions to 9(h). In actual practice, the

The veto message referred to Truman's efforts in 1945 to gain voluntary agreement between labor and business leaders. In vetoing the bill, he was seeking to avoid what he called "the most serious economic and social legislation of the past decade" and a "clear threat to the successful working of our democratic society."[4]

The president was not objecting to new legislation. He recalled that in his State of the Union message of January 1947 he had "recommended a step-by-step approach to the support of labor legislation." He added that there "is still a genuine opportunity for the enactment of [unspecified] appropriate labor legislation this session."[5]

Truman objected to the right-to-work Section 14(b) not because it violated established union security protections – this section actually was designed to ensure a compulsory open shop – but because it abandoned "the principle of uniform national policy under Federal law." He predicted a rash of such state laws: "This is not only an invitation to the States to distort national policy as they see fit, but is a complete forsaking of a long-standing constitutional principle."[6] Apparently it did not occur to him that this declaration of "constitutional principle" was in direct conflict with his acceptance of the principle of barring "communists" from elections to leadership positions or, through his loyalty order, from the workplace altogether.

Truman here exhibited a keen understanding of moderate labor leaders'

---

communists showed a wide range of reactions to the section. Some Communist Party members publicly quit the party but continued in their elected or appointed jobs. Most, I would guess, remained CP members and quit their union jobs.

In 1959, Congress tightened the 9(h) restrictions with a substitute section incorporated in the Labor-Management Reporting and Disclosure (Landrum-Griffin) Act. Effective September 14, 1959, this new act explicitly mentioned "political strikes" as a danger to the country and specified that it would be a crime for a member of the Communist Party to serve as an officer or as an employee of a labor union (except in a clerical or custodial position). It was under the Landrum-Griffin Act that the U.S. Supreme Court ruled that this substitute provision was unconstitutional – a bill of attainder – and said further: "The designation of Communist Party membership cannot be justified as an alternative 'short hand' expression for the characteristics that render men likely to incite political strikes" (Ann Fagan Ginger and David Christiano, *The Cold War Against Labor* [Berkeley, Calif.: Meiklejohn Civil Liberties Institute, 1987], pp. 437ff.). The Court went back to its own *American Communications Assn. v. Doud,* which had found Section 9(h) of Taft-Hartley to be constitutional. The Court now wrote that that case did involve a bill of attainder. As I understand this, the U.S. Supreme Court seems to have decided in 1959 that Section 9(h), which it upheld in 1948, was indeed a bill of attainder. In any case, the "loyalty" or "noncommunist" sections in both bills were now null and void. However, in the period under review, Section 9(h) was often a decisive factor in the policy debates of major unions.

[4]Veto message, p. 11.
[5]Ibid.
[6]Ibid., p. 10.

sensitivities as well as a strong protective instinct for his own political pre-rogatives. He voiced concern that H.R. 3020 would take the conciliation program out of the Department of Labor and turn it into an independent agency. By making the point that this bill went contrary to an agreement between labor and management to strengthen the conciliation program, Truman was simultaneously appealing to orthodox labor and expressing strong disagreement with H.R. 3020's removal of that function from his Department of Labor.

This president was a political animal. His emphasis on the change in the conciliation service should not be seen as disconnected from his other political instincts, including the labor votes he sensed he needed to win the 1948 election.

By standing firm on the conciliation function, he could show union leaders his concern for maintaining "their" U.S. Department of Labor intact; he could also show industry that he was complying with the desires it expressed in 1945 for traditional voluntarist, market-based bargaining.

Whatever Congress' or the president's motives, there is no small irony in the fact that the man chosen by Secretary of Labor Lewis Schwellenbach to direct the conciliation function and to strengthen the Labor-Management Conference mandate, Edgar L. Warren, became a victim of both Congress' hostility to the department and the president's loyalty order. In 1947, Congress let its distrust of unionism spill over into persecution of the entire U.S. Department of Labor. As the department's historian wrote in later years:

A good example of the crucifixion of a Department of Labor oriented toward the labor movement came during the conservative Eightieth Congress in 1946, when many congressmen opposed the programs of the Department in any shape, manner or form. As Ewan Clague, then commissioner of Labor Statistics, explained, employers distrusted both the Secretary of Labor and the Conciliation Service.[7]

President Truman was courting the chairman of the Senate Foreign Relations Committee and president of the Senate, Arthur Vandenberg, now more than ever an important ally for his international policies. But he found little sympathy in the Republican-led Congress for either his ambivalent labor policy or his Labor Department. This was owing in part to resentment against the handful of former New Dealers. For example, Ed Warren, the conciliation director, became a special "pinko" target of congressional Red-baiters partly

---

[7]Jonathan Grossman, *The Department of Labor* (New York: Praeger, 1973), p. 248. Grossman was the historian of the U.S. Department of Labor through the 1960s and into the 1970s.

because of Truman's own loyalty order. But there was now a general animus against this department because of its presumed concerns about class and gender:

And, indeed, the Eightieth Congress denuded the Department of Labor, leaving it like a plucked chicken. Congress began by removing the Conciliation Service – a function that had been placed in the original Department of Labor in 1913 – from the Department. Congressman Keefe also tried to cut out entirely the $300,000 budget of the Women's Bureau.[8]

Along with these congressional attacks during the immediate aftermath of Taft-Hartley, the administration was buffeted by a new barrage of employer propaganda against alleged union power and supposed pro-union governmental policies. The states were rapidly adopting right-to-work laws, often alongside their own state loyalty programs. At the federal level, the old-line employer associations that had made their reputations as opponents of unionism – notably the National Metal Trades Association and the National Association of Manufacturers – were expanding their budgets and pursuing the old objective of union-free workplaces. An additional and successful thrust against unions and their alleged supporters in government was being carried out by the Chamber of Commerce of the United States. Once Eric Johnston quit as president of the organization, in 1946, the Chamber assumed a leading role in influencing opinion makers, in and out of Congress, against all "socialist" entities – in which the Chamber included the Scandinavian countries, the United Kingdom, and reformers in the USA. If one may judge from literature issued by this important, deeply rooted association, the business community was not impressed by Truman, his loyalty order, or his veto.

The central feature of a series of antisocialist, anticommunist pamphlets distributed by the Chamber of Commerce in the late 1940s was the alleged power of "disloyal" people in unions and in government. My informed guess, from conversations with Trumanites on Capitol Hill and at the White House, is that these themes strongly influenced the president in the matter of his loyalty order. Ironically, the Chamber seemed to be convinced that it could not count on a Democratic president or a pluralist democracy. It offered as a model for grass-roots political action the series of articles by "John Sentinel" in the Milwaukee *Sentinel* designed to show that the United States could not absorb a radical labor union. That series is cited in *Communist Infiltration* (1946) as "an outstanding illustration of an exposure." The pamphlet tells

[8]Ibid.

employers how they could locate and promote "pro-American" labor leaders if and when they were required to deal with a union.[9]

The American Federation of Labor

All of these actions – President Truman's veto, organized employer propaganda campaigns, and congressional investigations – had an impact not only on policy makers in government but on labor leaders. The American Federation of Labor was attuned to both the ideological impulse behind Taft-Hartley and the change the law demanded for its own survival and adaptation.

In the early spring of 1947, daily AFL news releases carried a box declaring AFL opposition to the pending Taft-Hartley bill. The proposed law was perceived in some sectors as a renewed if still unarticulated threat to traditional AFL bargaining systems. The AFL was concerned about several Taft-Hartley clauses legalizing the injunction, as well as clauses restricting union security. It was probably also unhappy with new bars against foremen and supervisors, many of whom had been members of AFL-affiliated unions. These sections among others seemed to threaten the Federation's established collective bargaining practices.

Yet the AFL was not preparing a political counteroffensive. Though aware of Taft-Hartley's potential threat, the AFL leadership was not in any mood to encourage a united front with the CIO or other organizations. Although the CIO would have been a natural ally for a political counterattack, the AFL had doubts about the labor-law issue, having in a sense initiated the battle against the Wagner Act for its alleged favoritism toward the industrial form of unionism. Besides, in 1947 the old rivalry in recruiting the unorganized still separated the AFL and the CIO despite some early signs of ideological and political convergence. On top of all these differences, Sidney Hillman, as architect and leader of the CIO Political Action Committee, had added insult to injury by inviting participation from all sorts of radicals and New Dealish types in his political alliances.

Having helped defeat the employers' postwar offensive during the great strike wave of 1946, the AFL was confident of its future, Taft-Hartley or no

[9]Published by the Chamber of Commerce of the United States. Peter Hanlon Irons ("America's Cold War Crusade: Domestic Politics and Foreign Policy, 1942–1958" [doctoral dissertation, Boston University, 1972], p. 93) considers this pamphlet and others in the widely circulated series of Chamber pamphlets to have been a major factor in the issuance of Truman's loyalty order.

Taft-Hartley. Its members were enjoying standards of living higher than pre-war levels; full employment seemed at hand. Home ownership was common; even college for the kids was now a real possibility. And despite new govern-ment controls, the Federation seemed strong enough to grow – indirectly through its affiliates and directly through the so-called federal labor unions. So the AFL faced the Taft-Hartley Act with confidence. Although it had encouraged demonstrations against the "slave-labor" bills and generated nega-tive press stories about the new law, the AFL decided to comply.

At the convention of 1947, the delegates voted for affidavit signing and use of the NLRB. Once the convention accepted the executive council recommen-dation, there was really no longer a serious chance of repealing the new act. The AFL, as well as the CIO, continued to make repeal gestures; joint under-takings to halt new state and federal restrictions were mounted. And both federations kept up a stream of rhetoric about labor resistance. But, as they demonstrated at the 1947 convention, the AFL's leadership had already de-cided that there was an advantage in signing the affidavits. This was of course a major change in AFL political philosophy. The historical irony of that decision seems to have escaped the council majority. The decision ran counter to decades of opposite approaches by the AFL: antagonism to government intrusion in general and, specifically, to the National Labor Relations Act and the old NLRB.

John L. Lewis held out against compliance and affidavit signing. This executive council member and vice-president argued for "free" or laissez-faire bargaining and took his stand against what he considered a threat to democrat-ic rights. Whereas Lewis considered Section 9(h) to be dangerous governmen-tal intrusion, he affirmed his own and the miners' deep hatred of the statism of the Soviet Union's Communist Party. Though he may have been bolstered in these anti-affidavit views by the unusual market power of the UMWA – where a single picket could still close a pit and keep out scabs – Lewis publicly took his stand against compliance based on what he considered potential and in-tended damage to labor.

He charged at the 1947 AFL convention that the ruling majority on the executive council let itself be drawn into the affidavit controversy, which he considered a diversion from the many substantive threats in the law. The council majority, he said, was concocting a "political broth" that would lead the "lions" (rank-and-file members) to an unnecessary capitulation to employ-ers. He urged the delegates to defy the council "asses" who would lead them along a path to fascism: The act was replete with traps, he said, but only the affidavit signing "occupied the minds of our leaders and the press." Equating affidavit signing with compliance, he reiterated the philosophical stand he had taken at the Labor Management Conference of 1945, when the Miners were still unaffiliated. Lewis said then that labor did not need the government. Thus, Lewis remained consistent in his philosophical stand with respect to labor law.[10]

In giving the executive council's case, George Meany noted, somewhat ambiguously, that the bill had undergone "considerable modification before becoming Public Law 101." Despite his placatory point, the formal resolution adopted by the 1947 convention condemned H.R. 3020. The resolution, proposed by the Law Committee (headed by executive council member David Dubinsky of the International Ladies Garment Workers' Union), accused many Republicans in Congress, along with the southern poll-tax Democrats, of having sought "to discourage and sabotage collective bargaining itself." The "bill-of-rights" formula publicized by Hartley and Taft was seen as a fraud: Taft-Hartley, the resolution declared, was part of a plan "being developed and pushed by the National Association of Manufacturers."[11]

Despite this official denunciation, the AFL was not ready to mobilize its considerable political power for repeal. The Federation seemed mesmerized by the issue of communism, as were Congress and the president. When William Green testified to Congress on behalf of the AFL, he made clear that the Federation did not object to ridding workplaces of Reds. Reiterating the AFL's faith in collective bargaining in a market economy, Green told Congress that the Federation was prepared to rid business of "communist" workers, going beyond what Congress was contemplating in Section 9(h):

MR. MACKINNON [R., Minn.]: Would you see anything wrong in protecting an employer who had discharged a man because he was a Communist?
MR. GREEN: You are talking about employing Communists? Would he discharge a man who is a Communist? That would be a case to take up with a committee between union and management, and the union, if he is found to be a Communist, is not going to defend him.[12]

Like most labor leaders, Green was an advocate of democracy and "free" trade unionism. He undoubtedly realized that an open pluralist society favored the development of genuine trade unionism and collective bargaining. But while President Green favored democracy, he was also intent on demonstrating that the AFL drew the line against permitting alleged communist workers

[10]AFL Convention, San Francisco, 1947, *Proceedings*, p. 483.
[11]Ibid., p. 484.
[12]U.S. Congress, House, Committee on Education and Labor, 80th Cong., 1st sess., *Amendments to the National Labor Relations Act*, vol. 3, p. 1726.

– even if the charges originated with the employers – to keep their jobs and enjoy the advantages of the American Constitution and America's democratic political process.

There was also a nonideological, more practical reason for compliance, which Green's number-two colleague, George Meany, stressed at the AFL convention. The transcript of the proceedings shows Meany making frequent references to communism as a menace. His record was clear on that point. Yet Meany's main argument for affidavit signing was more practical. He cited the protection needs of the federal labor unions: "This proposition before the Convention has one purpose, and one purpose only," Meany said in opposing Lewis' proposal to boycott the NLRB. Compliance was necessary, he said, "to give the federal labor unions the opportunity to exercise their option under this law and to qualify by signing the non-Communist affidavit and meeting the law's other requirements if they so desire."[13]

This argument, coming from the secretary-treasurer, appealed to the public and the delegates. Who could say no to helping relatively vulnerable workers as well as assuring a flow of dues payments? The unstated argument, known to the council, organizers, and staffers, was that the federal labor unions were in competition with the CIO for factory-type workers; that John L. Lewis still controlled District 50 of the United Mine Workers, which was a catchall for recruiting and had a potential for upsetting traditional craft-exclusive jurisdictions. (It should be noted that in pre-CIO days the communist left found the federal labor union mechanism useful for bringing unorganized workers under some form of union protection as a means of sparing those workers from craft atomization.)

The majority on the executive council prevailed. After an extended discussion, delegates voted overwhelmingly for what amounted to compliance. While observing traditional autonomy – the resolution adopted by the convention stated that each affiliate could decide for itself whether to sign and file – the constitutional change brought the central AFL into compliance, overcoming an NLRB ruling that all officers of a federated labor body must sign. The 1947 convention change provided that the affidavits were to be signed by the two full-time officers, Green and Meany, and not by the international vice-presidents (including Lewis) who held honorific titles while representing their unions on the council. This arrangement – that only Green and Meany were to be considered officers – appears to have been cleared in advance with the general counsel and de facto boss of the new NLRB, Robert H. Denham.

[13]*Proceedings*, p. 2202.

In sum, the crucial political decision made at this convention was that the AFL would accept the new basic labor law of the United States. At the same time, the AFL decided to get more deeply into politics. It created its first year-round political machinery, Labor's League for Political Education (LLPE), as a direct result of Taft-Hartley.[14] In turn, the LLPE became a significant force on behalf of Truman's 1948 reelection. Later, in 1951, the building trades unions launched their own gigantic legislative political action campaign to restore the status quo ante on construction sites by a "situs" amendment. Following the 1947 convention, Harry Truman was given de facto support for 1948, partly because of his veto, partly because of his promise to repeal Taft-Hartley. The Federation continued its now subdued rhetoric against Taft-Hartley. But the AFL and the vast majority of affiliates henceforth pursued a policy of affidavit signing and compliance.

Although the AFL decided to sign and comply, the United Mine Workers did not. The printers (ITU) also abstained. Immediately following the convention vote, Lewis again withdrew the Mine Workers from the Federation, with the previously mentioned dramatic flourish, announcing his disaffiliation in a four-word scrawl: "Green, we disaffiliate. Lewis."[15]

Referring to the rhetorical opposition that the AFL had pursued, George Meany told his official biographer a few decades later, "We sort of over-reacted. The proof is that we have made progress." The executive council's rhetorical opposition and complacency, as well as its real but temporary concerns, were all captured by Philip Taft in interviews he conducted with executive council leaders for his 1948 study:

The Taft-Hartley law has reintroduced the injunction in labor disputes although the Government alone has the right to appeal for such orders. This may enable a hostile chief counsel of the National Labor Relations Board to harass unions and impede their legitimate functioning. Up to now, 1948, the law had not had a very serious effect upon the trade unions. Recognition of the right to organize by a conservative Congress is an indication of the long distance we have travelled since the 1930s [the era] of the "open shop" (p. 596).

Taft did not allude to the organizational impulse toward compliance. In Chapter 4, I referred to the AFL Pattern Makers' satisfaction with Taft-Hartley. This was no idiosyncratic reaction. This union's acceptance explains

[14]Interview with Joseph Keenan, first LLPE director, January 2, 1968, Washington, D.C., in Irving Richter, *Political Purpose in Trade Unions* (London: Allen & Unwin, 1973).
[15]This was written on a scrap of paper 6″ by 9″, rather than on the usual letterhead. One can see it as a further expression of Lewis' contempt for the AFL and for the ex-coal miner who headed the AFL at the time. This withdrawal slip is in the AFL-CIO George Meany Memorial Archives in Silver Spring, Md.

to a significant degree why the executive council of the AFL was ready not only to accept but to press for compliance. The Pattern Makers' Union from its beginning was the archetypal craft union, made up of skilled artisans, the type that had been the foundation for the American Federation of Labor since Gompers. It should be recalled that in 1938 the executive council had aligned itself with the Republicans and their allies, the southern poll-tax Democrats led by Representative Howard W. Smith of Virginia, for a legislative campaign to amend the Wagner Act so that craft unions would be protected against the CIO's industrial thrust. Thus, as Gross has put it, Taft-Hartley was, in a sense, the victory sought by the AFL in 1938. The authors of the final Taft-Hartley bill incorporated the old AFL demand for craft protection, a section known as "appropriate unit" for labor-board elections. Henceforth, the crafts would be enabled to have separate elections. The Pattern Makers' pride of craft and competition with the industrial unions seem to have been the decisive factors in the de facto decision of that AFL-affiliated craft union to comply rather than do a "John L. Lewis thing," that is, reject the new law.

Although George Q. Lynch, the Pattern Makers' general president, was one of the few executive council members who disapproved of the attack on the Wagner Act, Lynch's successor in the same AFL national union told me that Taft-Hartley "saved" the Pattern Makers from the CIO: "We are the first link in the production chain," Mr. Gunnar Hollstrom said with obvious pride of craft:

We cut the wood patterns for production tools. Under the old NLRB we were always being outvoted by the production workers. We had to keep our elbows out all the time to protect our interests. When Taft-Hartley came along, we first wanted to have nothing to do with it. We were going to do a John L. Lewis thing. I was then MidWest secretary. But I knew, and Lynch knew, that if we didn't take advantage of the law, we would be swamped and maybe go down the drain. Sure, we did talk about the slave-labor law. Our journal always denounced it. At the same time, we did sign the affidavits. We did use the law. We knew once we got on the ballot our boys would come out and vote, and vote for the Pattern Makers. After all, there was about sixty cents an hour difference in the wages we negotiated. So we got to do the bargaining. Our craft was saved. Yes, sir! Taft-Hartley saved us.[16]

[16]Interview at Hollstrom's home, Naples, Florida, January 2, 1979. President Lynch retired in 1960. Prior to that, according to George Meany, Lynch opposed the creation of the Industrial Union Department in the merger of the AFL and the CIO in 1955 because he feared, again according to George Meany, that the crafts would be "submerged" by the IUD (Archie Robinson, *George Meany and His Times* [New York: Simon & Schuster, 1981], p. 177). Lynch also opposed any no-raiding agreement with the CIO, again for fear of what that would do to the craft he represented, according to Hollstrom.

Similarly, while arguing against continuation of the Taft-Hartley provision requiring a membership vote to obtain or maintain a union shop (a provision that was dropped after many costly, time-consuming victories by unions), Louis S. Belkin of the AFL International Chemical Workers' Union also recognized the actual help his members gained under the craft-separation clause of the law. After enactment, he told a Senate committee: "It, that provision of Taft-Hartley, has given us an opportunity to reorganize our locals and to re-cement unity within them. We have been given a stronger bargaining platform for negotiations with management."[17] In short, competition with industrial unionism, not opposition to Taft-Hartley, motivated some AFL-affiliated unions and perhaps the AFL itself, despite rhetoric from the AFL and its affiliates signifying opposition to the law.

CIO Unions in the Aftermath of Taft-Hartley

Much of the CIO's behavior in the aftermath period can be explained by the new political climate. In practice, the CIO was behaving quite differently than its rhetoric might suggest. While this once militant labor center continued some New Dealish behavior, it too was essentially adapting to the current political climate and legal framework. This conforming behavior in turn was bringing the CIO into ideological convergence with the AFL, first demonstrated in somewhat similar convention actions in 1947, and followed by joint political campaigning in 1948 and a common ideological thrust in 1949 for the creation of a new world labor body, the anticommunist and anti-WFTU International Confederation of Free Trade Unions (ICFTU).

In writing about the contemporaneous views of labor leaders regarding Taft-Hartley, Philip Taft said they had a "case against fighting [legal] disavowals of Communist leaning," not, he wrote, because of their acceptance but because "many sections of organized labor have been among the bitterest opponents of Communism in the United States." He also saw "real politics" emerging from labor.

Labor's tired rhetoric about the "slave-labor" law remained. But within the AFL and CIO in late 1947 and into the 1948 presidential campaign, political motion was almost entirely directed toward preservation and consolidation of the leadership status quo, under the guise of testing "loyalty." This spurious

---

[17]Cited by Harry A. Millis and Emily Clark Brown, *From the Wagner Act to Taft-Hartley* (Chicago: University of Chicago Press, 1950), p. 537.

type of politics is captured in a 1985 history of AFL and CIO activity in a labor stronghold, the State of Ohio. Although the two federations were rallying behind Truman because of "his and the Democratic Party's opposition to the Taft-Hartley Act," the 1948 election "became a litmus test of loyalty":

> For CIO leaders – most of whom supported the re-election of President Truman, because of his and the Democratic Party's opposition to the Taft-Hartley Act – the election became a litmus test of loyalty. From national headquarters to local union halls, cleavages widened between Wallace-supporters opposed to the accelerating Cold War, and unionists convinced that such activists were actually tools of an international Communist conspiracy. Though Wallace was soundly defeated, conservative CIO officials marked his backers within the organization as disloyal to the union cause, as possible traitors to their country and, therefore, as targets for disciplinary action.[18]

In the State of Illinois, Joseph Germano, a prominent regional Steel Workers official, was elected president of the state CIO council in 1947; he promised publicly during his campaign that he would lead a fight to rid all affiliates of any communist interference and end "Communist domination," now a buzzword at national CIO headquarters. "I am not going to plead for unity," Germano added, "because any member or any union that puts foreign ideology above the No. 1 job of defeating the Tafts and the Hartleys is simply not deserving of our cooperation."[19] This was said on September 1, 1947, the very day Taft-Hartley became effective.

The periodization implied in the discussion above is far from definitive. Still, in 1947 and 1948, the national CIO, while ambivalent, was in favor of maintaining the status quo. In the CIO, I saw genuine political action against further legislative restrictions, but not for Taft-Hartley repeal. These unions saw threats from three separate forces. First, there was the formidable right-to-work movement, spearheaded by a National Right-to-Work Committee, which had become so well funded that it could hire Fred Hartley of Taft-Hartley fame as one of its first organizers. Hartley's job was to promote state right-to-work laws for a (compulsory) union-free environment, as authorized by Section 14(b). Along with political efforts to stop state right-to-work laws, the national CIO leadership, like the strategists of the AFL, perceived that an equally serious threat emanated from the unpredictable Progressive Party and its presidential and vice-presidential candidates, Henry Wallace and Senator Glen Taylor of Idaho. For Murray, his man Germano in Illinois, his people in

---

[18]Raymond Boryczka and Lorin Lee Cary, *No Strength Without Union: An Illustrated History of Ohio Workers, 1803–1980* (Columbus: Ohio Historical Society, 1985), p. 249.
[19]*CIO News*, September 2, 1947, p. 2.

Wisconsin, and his allies in Ohio, this threatened the CIO's historic alliance with the White House.

Both the AFL and the CIO seemed complacent about the new labor law, in part because of its favorable prospects for successful bargaining. They were also subdued by the notion of incurring the wrath of the White House and Congress during the Great Fear, so they stayed in line with the act. Certainly the House Committee on Un-American Activities (HUAC) understood how well the fear of being labeled a subversive worked to its advantage.

One HUAC star witness, Whittaker Chambers, has suggested how general and pervasive was the fear of communism among all Americans in this post–Taft-Hartley, pre-McCarthy period. While Chambers did not discuss Taft-Hartley or labor leaders per se, he may have been more accurate than we in the CIO were prepared to admit about the fear that "the mass of Americans" felt about the "triumphs of Communism." Whittaker told the House committee and the country that

Communists or close fellow travellers or their dupes otherwise undefined, working in the United States Government or in some singular unofficial relationship to it, or working in the press, affected the future of every American now alive, and indirectly the fate of every man now going into uniform: their names, with half-a-dozen exceptions, still mean very little or nothing to the mass of Americans. But their activities, if only in promoting the triumphs of Communism in China, have decisively changed the history of Asia, of the United States, and therefore the whole world.[20]

At the time, I not only ignored this aspect of U.S. politics but exaggerated the opposition to the new labor law. In April of 1947, I wrote a column for my readers on Phil Murray's and William Green's denunciations of Taft-Hartley and their fears of new, more restrictive laws. I was really saying what they ought to fear. I was implying unity, not fragmentation. Neither I nor CIO publicists wished to publicize the fact that all the influential employer associations were on the offensive; that the AFL and the CIO, far from being defiant, were in agreement with the main thrust of the employers' propagandists in publicly fighting "socialism" and "communism"; that this new labor harmony was really in tune with the Truman administration. Though in an ideal world the AFL and the CIO would have united against Taft-Hartley, I now realize what was not so evident at the time, namely, that Murray and Green had dissimilar views on Taft-Hartley, even though they held generally converging political views, particularly on the 1948 presidential election. Had I discussed the real

[20]U.S. Congress, House, Committee on Un-American Activities, *Hearings*.

AFL/CIO differences, I would have had to concede that despite their ideological stand – against all forms of radicalism – institutional conflicts remained and overshadowed considerations of class within the labor movement.

When Taft-Hartley repeal became a possibility after Truman won reelection and Congress was recaptured by the Democrats, labor froze in its tracks. Gus Kelley, a key member of the House Committee on Education and Labor, wrote to a UE official in his district lamenting that labor in the person of AFL and CIO representatives, was showing no interest in repeal.

I also ignored a great religious upsurge, spearheaded by the Catholic Church, that was accompanying the shift in political climate.[21] I saw this upsurge occurring in my own union, the United Auto Workers, and throughout the CIO, when the Association of Catholic Trade Unionists assumed leadership of the right-wing caucuses. The Church's historic role in unions was to prevent a class-conscious labor movement. Since 1937, the ACTU's focus had been to oust labor's "Reds" from the CP-influenced industrial unions (e.g., UE, UAW) and from the major industrial councils in New York, Ohio, Wisconsin, California, and other left strongholds. For this purpose, the ACTU was pushing Phil Murray into taking a more active political posture, not against Taft-Hartley but against the communist minority that had been able to survive the act.

Monsignor Charles Owen Rice, Phil Murray's parish priest in Pittsburgh, was probably the single most important leader in the aftermath years up to 1952 within the Roman Catholic Church and the ACTU. Rice has described his efforts and the strategy guiding the ACTU within some CIO unions for pressuring Philip Murray:

This anti-Communism was hard work. For the most part, the rank-and-file was non-ideological and was interested in bread and butter, which the Leftist leadership provided as well as any, and better than most. . . . I assure you that I was pushing Murray to move against the Communist power, rather than the reverse.

Rice discerned the elastic quality of the issue and the long-range impact on the UAW and UE and, through these two affiliates, on the CIO:

A word about my use of the words, Communist and Communistic. It is deliberate, if not always accurate. The issue was whether or not men in the trade union movement and its leadership were to be permitted to profess Communism or support it. Then I thought no, now I think yes. . . . In those days, the Communists were not models of tolerance themselves, and chewed up their opposition when they could. Nevertheless,

---

[21]A prominent noncommunist leftist critic of labor, Sidney Lens, did not mention the subject of Catholicism in his popular *Unions: And What They Do* (New York: Putnam, 1968). The subject is rarely discussed in labor histories.

the American trade union movement would be healthier today if Phil Murray had not purged the CIO and if a strong, broad-based Communist minority had been able to survive in the trade unions. The split of the UE was a loss and so was the transformation of the UAW into a monolith.[22]

In a more scholarly study of the ACTU and the Church, Douglas Seaton has pointed to the association's ambivalence toward Taft-Hartley and its constant crusade against the left. At the hearings stage, Seaton noted that the ACTU's reactions were "ambiguous and modest." But after passage, the ACTU's "main goal" was not repeal or compliance but defeating the communists. So the ACTU pressed (and won wide CIO agreement) for both "cultivation and pressuring [of] centrist leaders like President Philip Murray and the encouragement of 'raiders' against 'non-complying affiliates.'"[23]

Lewis Dips Into CIO Dissenters' Waters

While the CIO continued to split over Section 9(h), John L. Lewis independently resumed his stand against Taft-Hartley compliance at a June 23, 1951, outdoor meeting sponsored by Local 600, UAW-CIO, the largest local in the CIO, at Ford's gigantic River Rouge plant.

[22]Monsignor Charles Owen Rice, "The Tragic Purge of 1948." This article appears in an obscure (mimeographed) newsletter, *Blueprint: For the Christian Reshaping of Society* (Loyola University, New Orleans), February 1974, pp. 1–5. Ronald W. Schatz, *The Electrical Workers: A History of Labor at General Electric and Westinghouse* (Champaign: University of Illinois Press, 1983), pp. 181–3, makes the important point that the ACTU, which he shows playing a central role in the right-wing caucuses of the UE, was related to, but wholly different in orientation from, the Catholic Worker movement headed by Dorothy Day in New York. ACTU policy was also ideologically opposed to such liberal Catholic prelates as Bishop Sheil of Chicago and Monsignor Haas of Washington, D.C.

[23]Douglas Paul Seaton, "The Catholic Church and the Congress of Industrial Organizations: The Case of the Association of Catholic Trade Unionists, 1937–1950" (unpublished doctoral dissertation, Rutgers University, 1975), p. 201. For a contemporaneous journalistic account, see the pamphlet *ACTU: The Catholic Church in the Labor Movement* published by *The Daily Compass* ("A [short-lived] New York Daily Newspaper for Liberal Americans of Every Race, Color and Creed"), 1940. The 600,000-strong UE – a special target of the ACTU – would shrink to about 50,000 after the CIO expelled it; or, as the UE officers later insisted, after it voluntarily withdrew from the CIO. The work of the ACTU and of Murray and his organizing staff, as well as congressional investigations and NLRB actions, all contributed to the decline. The split at the CIO arose over the Truman and Wallace campaigns, but the divisions over Taft-Hartley both followed and intensified these conflicts. Following the UE disaffiliation, the CP cadres in the UE, while reflecting the splits, also created further splits: Some members campaigned to affiliate with other mainstream unions, ranging from the UAW to the Teamsters, while others decided to go it alone and remain an independent international union. Cf. James J. Matles (one of three dominant UE top officers) and James Higgins, *Them and Us: Struggles of a Rank-and-File Union* (Englewood Cliffs, N.J.: Prentice-Hall, 1974), pp. 198ff. This UE-sponsored book claims that the UE was not expelled by the CIO; that it quit in 1949 by refusing to pay dues following CIO-encouraged raiding (pp. 195–6).

The local had already signed the affidavit, under prodding from the international and from local president Carl Stellato, who had recently become a dissident within the Auto Workers. Earlier in 1951, Stellato – with international union prodding – had launched his own vigorous prosecution, via local trials of five founding minor Local 600 officers, under terms of a rarely invoked anticommunist provision of the UAW constitution adopted in 1940. (The five were eliminated from their elected union positions.) However, by the time of Lewis' appearance, Stellato had become reconciled with the Communist Party left and the old but still strong left-center coalition that had built Local 600. This local had special reason to feel confident about its bargaining strength. Not only had it won an earlier NLRB election against the senior Henry Ford's violent opposition, but it had just scored a resounding majority in a post–Taft-Hartley NLRB-conducted poll that showed more than 90 percent in favor of maintaining the union shop at the Rouge plant. While the international hailed that election, it was not invited to endorse, and conspicuously refrained from any endorsement of, the Lewis affair.

Obviously conscious that he was still the revered former CIO chief, the aging Lewis opened his address with a cordial embrace of Stellato. He then took a swipe at the "boycott" of the celebration by the "pseudo-intellectual nitwit" UAW international union president. This was laughingly recognized by the audience as a slap at Walter Reuther and his recently negotiated escalator clause with General Motors providing an automatic cost-of-living increase in the hourly wage adjustable to the Bureau of Labor Statistics' price index. Through this contract, widely seen as an adjustment to price inflation, Reuther had seized the imagination of many rank-and-file members of the UAW and other labor sympathizers throughout the world. Lewis, however, visualized the escalator clause as a threat to the fundamentals of Mine Workers' traditional "private" collective bargaining. Having made his reputation in coal mining during periods of economic hardship and deflation, Lewis continued to make gains for coal miners as the economy improved. But he now took a more pessimistic view of the postwar economy, although he remained confident about the UMWA. Reuther, on the other hand, while certainly less confident of his union's power vis-à-vis the manufacturers, was clearly counting on a relatively full-employment economy, characterized by a rising cost of living due to price inflation. These factors would favor collective bargaining. Lewis was obsessed with the sliding scale that the coal operators had imposed on the coal miners in the prewar period to push wages down as coal prices fell. He therefore saw this GM agreement as a danger to miners and other workers.

Despite his well-known faith in the free-enterprise system, John L. Lewis said he saw "economic and social peril . . . not far down the road ahead." Like many others, Lewis was in error about the timing of the economic downturn, despite the relatively minor recession during the period immediately preceding his talk. He was more accurate about political repression. There is no evidence that he was the least bit alarmed about McCarthyism, but he warned his audience: "Compliance to the Taft-Hartley Act, which American labor did at the San Francisco Convention four years ago, was a throwback designed not to destroy labor as such in a forthright and immediate manner, but first to prevent the growth of unions as such."[24]

Of course, there is another, more personal explanation for Lewis' surprising appearance before a dissident UAW audience. He had always protected his dominant role in labor history, holding in contempt Phil Murray along with Walter Reuther and other CIO leaders, as well as AFL president William Green. In addition, he no doubt felt comfortable meddling in UAW-CIO internal politics because of his past role – as CIO president – in leading, financing, and signing the first contract with Ford for the young auto union.

Lewis knew that the Reuther brothers had been prominent in early CIO organizing. And, far from being an "intellectual nitwit," Reuther, now established as a world figure, was fully cognizant of labor strengths and weaknesses. He understood as well as any labor leader the workers' cultural, economic, and political possibilities at home and abroad. Lewis must surely have known that in addition to having risen to power in the UAW, Reuther was a likely candidate for the presidency of the CIO. Thus, Lewis was displaying some jealousy, an emotional response to "the Redhead's" fame. (By 1951, Reuther was getting as much publicity as Lewis had received in his heyday as CIO chief. Possibly because of his identification with labor's right wing, Reuther was getting far more favorable treatment from the major media than had Lewis.)

At the Dearborn meeting, Lewis apparently felt called upon to make his own contribution to the current fashion of Red-baiting, blasting Reuther for his youthful fling in an automobile plant in the Soviet Union in the early 1930s. Averill Harriman, the most prominent New Dealer remaining in the Truman administration and a vocal advocate of the Truman Doctrine, was also Red-baited, apparently because of his early efforts to secure diplomatic recognition of the Soviet Union.[25]

Like most of Lewis' actions, we see here no clear-cut objective beyond

---

[24]UAW Local 600, "Official Program of the 10th Anniversary Celebration," n.d., p. 13. Cf. Roger R. Keeran, *The Communist Party and the Auto Workers Unions* (Bloomington: Indiana University Press, 1980), pp. 218–22.
[25]"Official Program," p. 16.

trying to protect the miners' flank. Yet the episode was more than biographical gossip. Clearly, it was an act of courage in 1951 to appear at a public meeting denouncing the now broadly accepted loyalty oath. While Lewis saw the escalator clause as a threat to the miners, he did not shrink from discussing the aftermath of Taft-Hartley as he saw it in relation to employees in general. However, he was also opposed to Reuther's efforts to gain control of the UAW. Lewis, we can assume, saw that signing the affidavit had become central not only to Taft-Hartley policy but to control of this pivotal CIO affiliate. While Lewis avoided a direct confrontation on the matter of the Addes-Thomas-Leonard challenge to Reuther, he did so indirectly by repeating the emphasis he had given at the AFL convention to the Section 9(h) issue.

Whatever else Lewis' Local 600 appearance signified, it was widely seen in Detroit not as part of the struggle for repeal but primarily as one more development in the long saga of UAW factionalism.

In the remaining pages of this chapter, I will discuss the Taft-Hartley aftermath as seen from the perspective of internal and external politics in several representative CIO affiliates, including Local 600 along with the international UAW-CIO and its Local 248.

United Packinghouse Workers of America (UPWA, CIO)

I have previously discussed the legal impact of Taft-Hartley on the United Packinghouse Workers (see Chapter 4). This industry, one of the first to apply mass-production techniques, employed blacks, women, and thousands of unskilled and semiskilled workers. Under the CIO, the union became a stronghold of the Communist Party. Indeed, according to Saul Wellman, a former official coordinator of the Communist Party's industrial union activities, Herbert March, a Packinghouse executive board member, was one of four party members chosen to go public about his party membership shortly after the end of World War II, before Taft-Hartley went into effect. According to Wellman, this party decision came about to show the communists' representation and influence in industry and to show that the Communist Party was "the dominant influence in the Packinghouse Union."[26]

The communists and their supporters had deep roots in this CIO affiliate. It

---

[26]Interviews, Detroit, October 5, 1982, and Washington, D.C., November 2, 1987; cf. Jacqueline Jones, *Labor of Love, Labor of Sorrow: Black Women, Work, and the Family from Slavery to the Present* (New York: Basic, 1985).

was centered in Chicago, which was also headquarters of its arch-rival, the Amalgamated Meatcutters and Butcher Workmen of North America, AFL. Immediately after the CIO voted in late 1947 to leave to its affiliated internationals the decision about affidavit signing, this union's international executive board voted by a narrow margin to comply with the statute and with Section 9(h), requiring all four top officers to sign. Divisiveness on the board surfaced over the status of Herbert March, then still a board member. He was a hero of the CIO organizing years in the Chicago area, the most charismatic and well-known personality in the industry. It was unthinkable in this union that Herb March would be dropped from leadership. To protect March after Taft-Hartley was made into law, the board voted to make him Chicago district director, then voted that district directors were not officers and therefore not required to sign the affidavits. This was a short-lived compromise. Following a disastrous 1948 strike, the board decided it was vulnerable to raids from the AFL's meatcutters' union. So the board voted for full compliance. This meant that March would be dropped from the high councils of the union.

The Packinghouse Workers, rebuilt after the 1948 disaster, managed to avoid some of the more traumatic CIO splits. It did not retreat from its past militancy and tolerance of minority dissent. Roger Horowitz attributes this to the leadership of international president Ralph Helstein, "a liberal of the truest sort." The price, however, was accommodation to CIO political policy, including support for Truman in 1948 and acceptance of Taft-Hartley:

In 1948, the UPWA abandoned its position in favor of independent political action adopted in 1947, and endorsed Truman. However, in a typical manner, the convention did not make its ruling binding on all subordinate bodies of the UPWA, such as local unions and districts. Thus the left-wing District No. 1, based in Chicago, actively supported the Wallace campaign, and several Chicago leaders (such as Sam Parks from the Wilson Local No. 25) ran for office on the Progressive Party ticket.[27]

Moreover, Horowitz wrote, "Ralph Helstein indicated that he planned to vote for Wallace. I don't know if he actually did so."[28]

Herbert March was ousted in 1948 in the process of compliance with Taft-Hartley. The national union decided to sign the affidavits and get on the NLRB ballot against its AFL rival union. In short, despite Helstein's liberalism and the retention of left staffers and even an absence of "irrational anti-Communism," it appears the UPWA would not, or could not, withstand the

---

[27]Letter from Roger Horowitz (then a resident expert on the packinghouse industry and the CIO union at the Wisconsin State Historical Society in Madison) to Irving Richter, June 24, 1986.
[28]Ibid.

act. Yet in this instance, unlike the UAW (see below), the rank and file retained "control over local unions."

There were indeed differences in the UPWA model. In my view, however, the unusual retention of some democratic rights in this CIO affiliate in the aftermath of Taft-Hartley was due to a variety of features in the union and the industry. While Horowitz's two explanatory factors are plausible, I would add some additional personal factors and emphasize both the historical and institutional ones as well.

The UPWA conformed as well as resisted. The international took action to sign the affidavits on the heels of the 1947 CIO convention that permitted and encouraged such signing. As part of the pattern, one should also note that the international union ousted March from its high councils and accepted legal action against Olga Zenchuck, a local officer of the CIO Packinghouse Union in Detroit. In this respect, Helstein's union followed most affiliates in the Taft-Hartley aftermath. Though Helstein showed above-average tolerance of the left in general and known communists in particular, he voiced no known objection in 1952 when Zenchuck was indicted in a Detroit court for "making the false statement when as secretary of the CIO local here she was required to state whether she is or was a former member of the Communist Party." Although the Detroit representative of UPWA, Larry Roger, dissociated the international by saying Zenchuck had resigned "her Detroit office in 1950 or '51," she was indicted (at the initiative of the assistant U.S. attorney, Dwight K. Hamborsky) for having concealed her "Communist affiliation" in signing papers on October 20, 1949, as required "under the Taft-Hartley Labor Law."[29]

In addition to signing the affidavits, this international union under Helstein's leadership endorsed Harry Truman, the single most important criterion used by the national CIO after 1948 for deciding whether to put "communist-dominated" affiliates on trial.

An underlying reason for the UPWA's political exceptionalism in this period stems from the nature of the industry and its manpower policies. Upton Sinclair's novel *The Jungle* centers on the exploitation of diverse foreign-born workers to meet early production goals and to avoid unionization. And beginning with World War I, black workers from the South poured into the yards. By the 1940s, after years of turmoil, blacks had integrated the production lines and held leadership positions at all levels. Ethnic and racial diversity combined to make the union not only more tolerant than most, but more

[29]*Detroit Free Press*, January 21, 1953.

aggressive in demanding civil and constitutional rights. No CIO affiliate was more deeply involved, for example, in the fight to enforce Roosevelt's Fair Employment Practices Committee.

The great packinghouses, employing mainly unskilled and semiskilled workers, were largely open shops when the CIO came on the scene. Any questioning (by employers or employees) of minority political dissent was dismissed by union builders as disruptive. Stockyard employees flocked to the CIO not just for industrial organization but for the CIO promise of organizing "without regard to race, creed," etc. Even after the national CIO in 1946 began to frown on some outside organizations, some of which, notably the National Negro Congress, showed up on the attorney general's 1947 list as too "pink" or Red, the packinghouse affiliate continued to support community race-based activity.

International vice-president Russell Lasley, a black worker elected to the executive board of the UPWA early in the CIO era, was a rare but significant symbol of racial and political integration at the executive level well before other CIO unions had taken such a bold step. Blacks in the UPWA, Lasley told me in the early 1950s, were cognizant of their personal debts to the CIO for their achievement of dignity and recognition as well as job protection. "Through the CIO," Lasley said, he had increased his status in both the UPWA and the community. While Lasley himself did not enter politics, he met and talked with governors and presidential candidates and followed the progress of the National Negro Congress, which, he said, still received UPWA contributions.

Considering its history as well as its adaptation during the aftermath of Taft-Hartley, one can hardly dissociate this union's president, Helstein, from blacks and the left. Helstein was indeed an aberrant labor leader, an attorney who had risen to the presidency. A shrewd and gifted liberal, he approved of racial and political equality. Whatever his vote in the 1948 presidential campaign, he certainly made no public attack on Wallace or the Progressive Party, as the national CIO and other affiliates had. I believe he did vote for Wallace. Moreover, he continued to associate with radical attorneys and other liberals and radicals inside and outside labor, many of them Progressive Party campaign activists, including some who were closely associated with the Communist Party. On the other hand, he was shrewd enough to cultivate for his own protection not only Phil Murray but also some of the anticommunist leaders on the CIO executive board, notably Emil Mazey, elected secretary-treasurer of the UAW-CIO in 1947. Helstein carefully avoided head-on clashes with Phil Murray. He took pains to check with Murray on policy and personnel.

Finally, Helstein's behavior, which was distinctly different from that of other CIO leaders, cannot be entirely separated from his Jewishness. Historically, Jews in the labor movement had generally supported blacks' quest for equality.[30] As an enlightened Jew, Ralph Helstein might have joined the handful of his coreligionists who jumped on the Cold War bandwagon for their comfort and convenience. But he was deterred, as were many other liberal Jews, by the modern crusaders who often coupled their anticommunism with anti-Semitism.[31] I recall other CIO leaders who pointed out to me that Franklin Roosevelt had been duped by Stalin; that something had to be done to halt the "Jew-Bolshevik menace" seeping into the movies, the media, and government as well as into the labor movement. As a liberal, Helstein was indeed wary of McCarthyism. But as a Jew and a liberal, he was also reluctant to participate in any pogrom, be it against an unpopular religious minority or an unpopular political minority.

Yet the UPWA case seems to support the main argument of the present inquiry, namely, that the labor movement allowed itself to be diverted by the Taft-Hartley Act's anticommunist affidavit section. Even such a relatively tolerant affiliate of the CIO as the Packinghouse Workers was divided by 9(h) and contributed to the fragmenting of an already divided movement.

International Woodworkers' Association, CIO

The International Woodworkers' Association (IWA), CIO, resulted mainly from the indifference of the AFL's skilled membership to the organizational needs of the semiskilled and unskilled mill workers and lumberjacks. The union's historian notes that the IWA migrated from the United Brotherhood of Carpenters and Joiners, AFL, in 1937.[32] The membership of the IWA, spread more or less evenly across the United States and Canada, had as their first international president a Canadian communist and lumberjack, Harold Pritchett. In the early years of industrial unionism in logging and sawmilling, party affiliation was not a major issue. However, the IWA sensed that the boycott by the AFL Carpenters' union to halt the new CIO union presented a real danger. The AFL Carpenters' union's chief, "Big Bill"

[30]Hasea Diner, *In the Almost Promised Land: American Jews and Blacks, 1915–1935* (Westport, Conn.: Greenwood, 1977).
[31]This anti-Semitism surfaced even in the national CIO: at the 1947 convention and in correspondence from Nathan Cowan, chairman of the CIO National Legislative Committee. See letter from Cowan to Philip Murray, April 2, 1949, Murray Papers, Catholic University, Box 2.
[32]Jerry Lembcke, *One Union in Wood* (New York: International, 1984), ch. 20 ("Label Unionism Challenged"), pp. 301–13.

Hutcheson, was one of the most forceful opponents of the National Labor Relations Act. He publicly boasted of using the boycott to nullify NLRB certifications of the new mass-production union. In lieu of the Wagner Act, he had urged reliance on the boycott barring shipments from mills recognizing the IWA. While the AFL backed the Carpenters, the IWA was staking out under New Deal protection an egalitarian and internationalist philosophy incorporated in its original comprehensive charter: ". . . international in scope [the IWA] shall unite into membership all working men and working women who are employed in and around any operation or employment having to do with the processing and handling of wood products at all stages from the stump to the finished product."[33] Communists, Trotskyists, socialists, and Wobblies from the very start of this CIO affiliate (1936) held key positions, in both Canada and the States. Although the AFL boycotts had plagued the IWA from its beginnings, the new law, especially Section 9(h), vastly complicated the AFL split and also aggravated early IWA divisions.

The IWA joined many other CIO unions in thrusting "slave-labor" rhetoric into editorials, news stories, and speeches. Beneath rhetorical harmony, however, were strong ideological strains. Long before 1947, a right wing had formed. Known throughout the industry as the White Bloc, this group of IWA members had been working for the elimination of Harold Pritchett from the presidency. Pritchett had been the unquestioned leader of the "Red Bloc," or the left, which included Communist Party members from the United States and Canada.[34]

Here as elsewhere, there was a muting of the Red issue during the Second World War. Pritchett continued to lead the IWA from his own stronghold in British Columbia. But in 1947 he lost the election. At the 1948 Portland (Oregon) convention of the Woodworkers, both the Americans and Canadians were caught up in the stampede to comply with Taft-Hartley. As in many other unions, the real internal concern was not the act itself but the signing and filing of the 9(h) affidavits. Pritchett's successor as international president, James Fadling, had scored his first victory as candidate of the White Bloc by winning a majority vote on the international executive council for a motion that all officers, including the board members from Canada, should sign the

---

[33]Quoted in National Industrial Conference Board, *Source Book of Union Government Structure and Procedures* (New York: NICB, 1956), p. 328.
[34]In an article in the Canadian newspaper *The Herald* (British Columbia), January 21, 1975, p. 13, Chris Potter depicted Pritchett as a 92-year-old member of the Canadian Communist Party since 1931; Potter's article was entitled "Leading B.C. Labor Figure Tells How It Is – And Was."

affidavits. The 1947 convention concurred. Thereupon, as Fadling must have anticipated, three left-wing members of the council resigned. At this point, after the IWA decided to sign and the left quit the council, Pritchett led the British Columbia District out of the IWA and established the unaffiliated Woodworkers' Industrial Union of Canada, charging among other things that the Fadling–White Bloc leadership had been responsible for "signing of the 'yellow dog' Taft-Hartley anti-Communist affidavits."[35]

Thus, what the union later called the Taft-Hartley crisis split the IWA. The U.S. change of labor law caused both the expulsion of the left and the departure of the Canadian woodworkers, fragmenting a CIO union already weakened by AFL resistance and employers' anti-unionism. The IWA example supports the thesis that Taft-Hartley splintered the union movement, not over halting or repealing the act but over compliance with the noncommunist affidavit. After the leadership was no longer challenged, a 1963 article, "Democratic IWA Cleaned Out Communist Leader," appeared in *The International Woodworker:* "Although the rank and file now controlled the International Union, some district councils and local unions continued to have Communist troubles. Enactment of the Taft-Hartley Act provided means to clear some of these people [Communists] out of the union."[36] It will be seen that one important UAW-CIO figure also made that claim for Taft-Hartley. In this IWA instance, as in the UAW, the Taft-Hartley loyalty feature was supplemented by a constitutional ban on communists holding office. The two features combined were vital for achieving control "permanently," the incumbents revealed in a later historical account:

The non-Communist affidavit [was] rejected by Second Vice President Karly Larsen and Secretary-Treasurer Ed Laux of the International Union, so their resignations were demanded and received by Fadling, then International President. A sequel to this story was written in 1953, when the Western Washington District Council booted Larsen from his office of second vice president under the provision in the IWA Constitution that permanently bars a Communist from holding union office. . . . [The] greatest fight against Communists took place in 1948 and early 1949, when Pritchett-led forces attempted to lead the British Columbia District Council out of the IWA into their new Woodworkers Industrial Union of Canada after condemning the IWA at the district

---

[35]Lembcke, *One Union in Wood,* pp. 77ff. I am indebted to Professor Lembcke of Lawrence University, formerly research director of the IWA, for some of the background above. I had a general knowledge of the industry from my years in the U.S. Department of Labor, and published several articles on its southern, largely unorganized, sectors. I also spent a week in IWA headquarters in Portland, Oregon, in 1977, examining archives and interviewing Lembcke and other union officials. I continued my talks with Lembcke in subsequent years.

[36]*The International Woodworker* (organ of the International Woodworkers' Association), May 1963, pp. 2–3.

convention and railroading through a resolution demanding the recall of Fadling as president.[37]

The UAW-CIO

There were important similarities and differences between the Woodworkers and the international union the United Auto Workers. For the latter, one must delve again into the intricate and complex maze of UAW factional struggle in this period.

The auto workers' union was the crown jewel of the CIO. The UAW-CIO's international president, Walter P. Reuther, and his brothers, Roy and Victor, had been important in the CIO organizing years.[38] First elected president in 1946 and reelected in 1947, Walter Reuther was already world-famous for his innovative leadership. But he still lacked control over the subordinate structures and staff. This lack appears to be the key to UAW behavior in the aftermath period. The motivating factors behind the major actors in that struggle are given authoritative analysis in the 1988 biography of the UAW's veteran general counsel, Maurice Sugar. Like me, Sugar was discharged immediately after Reuther won control of the international executive board. Sugar put it this way: "Reuther combined the use of the anti-Communism that ran rampant in the Cold War era with acquiescence to the legal shackles now replacing the legal aid of the past."[39] It was not quite that simple.

Reuther continued to lead the UAW-CIO on the assumption that the economy was not going into depression or deep recession and that the political system would permit the functioning and growth of collective bargaining. Confident, hard-working, and persuasive, Reuther scored significant victories for the union's one-million-odd membership. He built a large new headquarters in Detroit, and in his term of office the UAW became known throughout the world as a model "social," broad-gauged labor union. My own narrow escape from discharge earlier in 1947 – a demand the international executive board at Louisville halted – clearly demonstrated that in early 1947 the international president was not yet in full control (see Postlude). However, as in the woodworkers' union, Taft-Hartley's loyalty provision gave the president of the huge international a powerful new weapon in his quest for a lasting and unchallenged power base.

When first elected in 1946, Reuther had a coalition behind him that could

[37]Ibid. (emphasis in original).   [38]Lens, *Unions*, pp. 34–5.
[39]Christopher H. Johnson, *Maurice Sugar: Law, Labor, and the Left in Detroit, 1912–1950* (Detroit, 1988), pp. 266–88.

defeat the strong left-center coalition despite Philip Murray's ongoing commitment to and friendship for the incumbent international president, R. J. Thomas. Thomas had been selected by Murray and Sidney Hillman – both CIO vice-presidents – back in 1939 to avoid a right-left schism in the auto union. The left had then briefly supported Addes to succeed the discredited Homer Martin in the presidency, but accepted the Murray-Hillman compromise. Murray remained formally committed to Thomas in 1946, as noted above, but wavered on the general idea of a united front that included the communists, who were behind Thomas. By late 1947, Murray, determined to rid the CIO of communist influence, was backed by the UAW right wing. But the right wing was still embattled with the left-centrists in the UAW-CIO. The new labor law, however, offered the youthful and vigorous leader of the right, Reuther, an additional means to eliminate that opposition. This emerges from a closer look at the international executive board and two UAW locals.

September 1947 Meeting of the UAW-CIO International Executive Board (IEB)

When the IEB met in September 1947, Taft-Hartley had not yet deeply affected the auto workers internally. The UAW's and the CIO's general counsels (Maurice Sugar and Lee Pressman, respectively) agreed that the new board should be ignored and the act resisted. In the UAW, while the majority agreed, the international president and his supporters advocated compliance under protest. Tensions were high. Walter Reuther was naturally ready to exercise the power of the presidency. But here he faced what he termed a mechanical majority that was determined to retain its own powers. This majority could and did check his policy-making and appointment powers, until in November of 1947 Reuther won a majority of the board. His core support was the well-organized and -financed Association of Catholic Trade Unionists' Detroit chapter. Following Reuther's victory, the ACTU became the main influence on the union for new administrative, appointment, and policy-making decisions (although the Reuther coalition continued to include a variety of trade unionists, including various anti-CP leftists and plain conservatives). The board's mechanical majority was jointly led by R. J. Thomas, who though defeated in 1946 had been elected international vice-president; and George F. Addes, long-time secretary-treasurer and widely regarded as the stronger of the two as well as more friendly to the left. Typical of the mercurial qualities inherent in UAW factional alignments, both Walter and Victor Reuther had from the start of the international been part of the left-center "unity caucus" from which they broke away only after a conflict within that caucus over Victor's race for the Michigan CIO presidency in 1938.[40]

Following the enactment of Taft-Hartley, the new labor law dominated the agenda at the September 1947 board meeting. All were in agreement that Taft-Hartley was an unmitigated curse and should be repealed. The divisive question debated was: What policy should be followed now that the law was in effect?

As previously indicated, opposing views were based on varying assessments of the CIO, the economy and its future, and collective bargaining philosophy. But the ghost at the board table was President Reuther's ongoing campaign to gain full control over the still turbulent UAW. The other three top officers, Vice-Presidents R. J. Thomas and R. T. Leonard and Secretary-Treasurer George F. Addes, as well as a majority of the regional directors, were all arrayed against him. It will be seen that Ford Local 600 and Allis-Chalmers Local 248 were also in the opposition camp.

The Reuther people were somewhat divided on tactics, though in agreement on the issue of compliance and the signing of affidavits. Richard Gosser, a frequent spokesman for the Reuther group, rose after a few of the group had expressed their pro–affidavit-signing positions, and proposed pressure on the national CIO president to win him over to a pro-compliance position:

I make a motion that we defer the subject matter of the Taft-Hartley Bill [*sic*] to the National CIO with the recommendation that in the convention they adopt the policy to allow each International Union to be autonomous within themselves as to whether they want to comply or not comply.[41]

Apparently Gosser, a conservative Ohio leader, sensed a growing tide within the CIO for compliance. Reuther did not support Gosser's motion. While he never lost sight of his primary goal of achieving control of the UAW, he wanted to avoid any appearance of public pressure on CIO president Murray. Reuther said he had made his own pro-signing position clear to Murray at a prior meeting of President Murray and the CIO vice-presidents. He later reported, prophetically, that he had said that while he could sympathize with Murray's "personal position, I believe that the majority of our [UAW] Board,

---

[40]Ibid., p. 268.
[41]UAW-CIO International Executive Board, September 1947, minutes, p. 179 (Archives of Labor History and Urban Affairs, Wayne State University, Detroit: UAW-CIO collection [hereafter ALHUA]).

if the International Unions in the CIO had an autonomous right to make a determination, would vote to comply. Such compliance," he said, "of course would be made under protest."[42]

The September IEB meeting took place only two weeks after the act became effective. In this transition period, the NLRB, the CIO, and many in the UAW were uncertain about what the NLRB guidelines for full compliance would be. Walter Reuther was determined to make affidavit signing on as broad a scale as possible a litmus test; and he was about to make compliance with Section 9(h) a major platform plank at the forthcoming UAW convention. But while his colleagues supported the Gosser amendment, Reuther made his opposition clear, deferring to Murray's "personal position," as did the mechanical majority. Gosser's motion was defeated. The UAW board simply decided to wait for the CIO convention scheduled for October. Maurice Sugar's advice to launch a fight against the new act was ignored, apparently because of Addes' lukewarm position on the issue.[43]

The 1947 convention did vote to permit affiliates to decide whether to sign and file affidavits. Most CIO affiliates took the convention vote as a signal to comply, despite Murray's objection to so doing. The delegates at the UAW-CIO November 1947 convention reelected Reuther and defeated Thomas, Leonard, and Addes. They elected a pro-Reuther majority to the board and enacted Reuther's major platform plank: a resolution accepting the necessity of compliance with the new labor law. His resolution included both affidavit signing and the obligatory call for repeal.

Walter Reuther's reelection was widely hailed as a major defeat for the CIO's left wing. Although Emil Mazey, his number-two running mate, was generally viewed in the CIO as a man of the left – an identification Mazey frequently confirmed – Mazey made affidavit signing the central platform policy in his successful race against George F. Addes.

A personal experience of mine at Emil Mazey's home local illuminated the polarization and fragmentation that took place within the UAW. Emil's brother, Ernest Mazey, who was a shop steward at Briggs Local 212, invited me to speak on Taft-Hartley. I narrowly escaped being asked to leave the Briggs Local 212 hall in August 1947 because I voiced my objections to the pro-compliance position publicly advocated that month – in advance of the UAW convention – by Emil Mazey. No sooner had I uttered this criticism than a motion was made by a local member, Jess Ferraza, with loud seconds from across the entire hall, to oust me from the hall on grounds of "impugning the

[42]Ibid., pp. 114ff.   [43]Johnson, *Maurice Sugar.*

integrity" of Emil Mazey, the local's former president. Had it not been for Ernest Mazey's intervention, I believe Ferraza's motion would have carried. Ernie Mazey's plea for the invited guest's free speech saved me and the UAW from what would surely have been a media spectacle of UAW splits on Taft-Hartley.

After the Mazey-Reuther team won out at the November 1947 convention, the UAW-CIO officially decided to accept the new federal controls. By voting for an affidavit-signing policy, the largest CIO affiliate fell in line with CIO policy as well as with the rival AFL's policy. Inside the UAW, this satisfied the large ACTU-based coalition that had formed around Reuther. In Washington, the new editor of the *CIO News* saw the UAW policy change, along with the election of an "anti-Communist majority" to the international executive board, as a severe defeat for the left.[44] As the new policy's proponents expected, the acceptance of Taft-Hartley compliance was accompanied by many voluntary and involuntary withdrawals of left-wing candidacies for local and regional office, by reinvigorated use of the international's constitutional provisions barring communist employees from union office, and the placing of international administrators over recalcitrant locals.[45]

The November UAW-CIO International Executive Board

In advance of the November 1947 convention, Reuther was so intent on compliance with the Section 9(h) affidavit that in October, before the board had a chance to act, he prepared a form for IEB members. At the convention he

---

[44]*CIO News*, 1947.
[45]After the sweep of top offices by Reuther, the defeated vice-presidents R. J. Thomas and R. T. Leonard were hired by Murray for the organizing staff of the national CIO. George Addes went into business for himself. Virtually all of the professional staff, including General Counsel Sugar and I, were immediately discharged.

I went to work in an Elyria plant as a buffer, after having turned down an offer made to me by A. F. Whitney of the Brotherhood of Railroad Trainmen at his estate near Cleveland to help him campaign for Harry Truman's 1948 reelection. I went to Detroit after being discharged by General Motors (for organizing, the regional director of the UAW, Paul Miley, publicly claimed; however, since the international refused to endorse the complaint against General Motors, we never learned whether the new NLRB would have ordered me reinstated). Returning to UAW haunts in Detroit, I worked briefly for the Michigan Wallace-for-President Committee. From that, I switched to campaign director for the Stanley Nowak-for-Congress Committee, a Democratic primary race against incumbent John Lesinski. After Nowak's defeat, I went into business for myself in Detroit. Hoping to continue working with the UAW and other unions, I chartered and became president of Organization Services, Inc. (OSI), in 1949. I stayed with OSI until 1962. I then left to study abroad, enrolling in 1963 at the University of Cambridge for my Ph.D. I began my teaching career at Mount Holyoke College in 1966 and in 1968 went to the University of the District of Columbia, then known as Federal City College. I retired from there in 1984.

urged them all to sign. Maurice Sugar's biographer has told of the decision by an otherwise "loyal Addes man," Arnold Atwood of Indianapolis, to "save his skin" by agreeing to sign even though the Addes majority had heretofore shown a united front in rejecting the proposal. Atwood's decision gave the Reuther group a board majority. In November, the constitutional convention made the Reuther pro-affidavit and pro-compliance position official union policy.

Whatever their motives, when delegates to the 1947 UAW convention voted for a policy of Taft-Hartley compliance, their action set the union's postwar course for labor relations within the new law. It gave scope for Walter Reuther's skillful leadership in bold new initiatives, including raiding of nonsigning CIO affiliates as well as new organization. Results aside, the point here is that the Reuther caucus' strong advocacy of affidavit signing was motivated mainly by internal electoral considerations. Thus Richard Gosser, now a putative vice-president of the international, declared during discussion of Section 9(h) that adoption of a pro-signing policy "would eliminate opposition to President Reuther." The board concurred. Paradoxically, new discord arose when the new majority voted not only to require the international officers to sign, but also to "instruct" the locals to do so.

When Cleveland board member Paul Miley asked the chair why local unions should be included, President Reuther replied that this was not "mandatory." Miley was referring to the absence of such a stipulation by the law. However, as seen from the example of two locals, a major push was made by the Reuther administration for signing and filing at local levels.

The new IEB that convened on November 10, 1947, was Reuther-controlled. That board, ready to place the union on a new path, had unmistakable evidence of both President Reuther's thoroughness and his anxiety to get the affidavits signed by locals. Each IEB member was presented with a printed form letter:

To: All Local Unions Having Pending NLRB Matters
Re: TAFT-HARTLEY COMPLIANCE

The preprinted signature on this letter was that of Emil Mazey, the new secretary-treasurer, who had campaigned on a pro-signing platform. He repeatedly told friends, off the record, that only Reds and their sympathizers objected to signing. While he was aware of Philip Murray's and John L. Lewis' objections, he and other speakers at the UAW convention emphasized they were for repeal of Taft-Hartley. The tone and wording of this postconvention letter makes affidavit signing urgent: "Compliance action should be completed before December 1, 1947."[46] In John L. Lewis' approach to Taft-Hartley at the AFL convention and again at the Local 600 commemorative meeting, he drew attention to the exaggerated emphasis on Section 9(h) affidavits. The same emphasis was evident in the UAW, where there were ideological and opportunist motivations for the compliance policy.

Reuther and Mazey indicated, in the above-mentioned UAW-CIO circular letter, that the international was not only favoring signing but was checking closely with the new labor board to assure compliance. "We have received assurance from the National Labor Relations Board that no UAW-CIO matter will be dismissed for failure to comply with the affidavits and reports requirements of the Taft-Hartley Act prior to that date [December 1, 1947]."[47]

To see how the international union UAW-CIO implemented its compliance policy against opposition locals, we revisit UAW Local 600, where Lewis spoke, and then go to Local 248, the centerpiece for the enactment of the "slave-labor" law in the House hearings.

Ford Local 600 (River Rouge)

At the Rouge plant, as elsewhere in 1947, the economy was showing signs of renewed vigor. The climate was generally favorable for collective bargaining. The UAW-CIO Ford Department and Local 600 were gaining new concessions from the Ford Motor Company for River Rouge workers.[48] Workers were buying their own homes in Dearborn, Detroit, and the suburbs. The Communist Party, however, was still relatively strong at this local and formed the core of a leftish, anti-Reuther coalition about as strong as the ACTU was in the right-wing coalition. The left-led "progressive" caucus had elected Tommy Thompson president. A June 1947 letter from Thompson to Reuther indicated how dangerous this local's opposition could be for the incumbents at Solidarity House. The Local 600 letter asked for a meeting with the international full-time officers (Reuther and Mazey) regarding "alleged raiding by the UAW against the Farm Equipment Workers (FE) at Fort Wayne, Indiana."[49] The FE had been for several years a well-known left-wing CIO affiliate and a strong competitor of the UAW in farm equipment. The FE was soon

---

[46]UAW-CIO International Executive Board, November 10, 1947, minutes, p. 25; circular letter (ALHUA).
[47]Circular letter (ALHUA).
[48]Robert M. McDonald, *Collective Bargaining in the Automobile Industry: A Study of Wage Structure and Competitive Relations* (New Haven, Conn.: Yale University Press, 1963), pp. 48–9, 138.
[49]UAW-CIO Local 600 Executive Board, June 30, 1947, minutes, p. 3 (ALHUA).

to be tried and expelled by the CIO as "communist-dominated." As of June 1947, however, Thomas and Addes visualized that union absorbed into the UAW as a potential partner of the anti-Reuther caucus. Like the officers of most left-wing unions, the FE's top officers had announced their refusal to sign the affidavits, thereby opening the way for UAW raids via NLRB-conducted elections. By acting in defense of the FE, Local 600 was clearly showing itself to be a source of serious opposition to international president Reuther.

All this dissent was seemingly stilled when Carl Stellato was elected local president in 1950, backed by Solidarity House and the ACTU-based right-wing coalition at Rouge – on a pro-signing, anticommunist platform. But the factionalism was amorphous and not nearly as neat as the left-right language may imply. Although Stellato in presiding at the 1951 Lewis meeting demonstrated a left-center reincarnation, he had as late as 1950 invoked the international constitution to try five dissident general council members at the behest of the international officers. The Local 600 general council was then a body that represented the sixteen or so buildings at Rouge and included all the officers of the local as a whole. Two of "the Five" were officers of the local. The other three were building presidents. The five men had been pioneer builders of the local union, had been in the forefront of Detroit demonstrations against the new law at the debate stages, and had led the opposition to affidavit signing in the general council and executive board.

In *WE ACCUSE,* a four-page printed tabloid issued by "the Five" during their local trial in 1950, Stellato and the international are pictured as the chief villains. In this written contemporaneous record, "the Five" refer to the labor law only peripherally. On the other hand, international representative Elisio "Lee" Romano, a former member of the progressive caucus at Local 600, told the House Committee on Un-American Activities in very specific language that "the Taft-Hartley thing" helped the right-wing caucus win election in 1950 (when Carl Stellato was their candidate) and that "the two people [apparently John Gallo and Bill McKie] who were on the staff of officers were forced to resign because they refused to sign the Communist affidavits. . . . In that sense," Romano explained, "the Taft-Hartley Act gave us a little success, let us put it that way."[50]

From this brief and incomplete account of actions and interactions at Ford

---

[50]U.S. Congress, House, Committee on Un-American Activities, *Hearings,* Detroit, pt. 2, March 11, 1952, pp. 2048ff. Romano here identified himself as a former member of the Communist Party at Rouge and an international representative of the UAW.

Local 600, one conclusion is clear: The international union was pressing compliance on the local to help the headquarters achieve centralized control and to ensure continuing aid from the federal government under the new law. Whatever the motives at Solidarity House and Local 600 under its rapidly shifting alignments, the result was to aggravate fragmentation both at Local 600 and within the Auto Workers. The substance of the Act was largely ignored once the local voted overwhelmingly and under Taft-Hartley balloting, for retention of the union security clause.

Allis-Chalmers Local 248: Disunity After Taft-Hartley

We have seen how centrally important a role Local 248 played in the House hearings on H.R. 3020. In the aftermath of enactment of the conference bill and its loss of the 1946–7 strike, this relatively obscure local of the UAW continued to occupy center stage within the union. Once again, Taft-Hartley compliance was a chosen path toward leadership consolidation at the international.

Founding president Harold Christoffel and his successor, Robert Buse, had been made scapegoats at the hearings not because of the bargaining they led but because of their political views. Both the local strike of 1946–7 and an earlier strike of 1940–1 were perceived as politically motivated work stoppages. After passage, Christoffel and Buse, as well as the local itself, continued to be victims at the hands of the executive branch of the federal government and the national leadership of their own international.

Immediately preceding congressional deliberations on the new labor law, in March of 1947 the Federal Bureau of Investigation, working in coordination with the House Committee on Un-American Activities, had been busy ferreting out "subversives" from various institutions, including Local 248, which the FBI and Congress saw as a key to UAW-CIO and CIO political policy.[51]

---

[51]As a result of recent lawsuits and Freedom of Information inquiries, we know that the FBI infiltrated not only Local 248 but many other institutions that Director Hoover regarded as radical: among others, the CPUSA, Martin Luther King's staff, and the Socialist Workers' Party. Previous discussion shows why and how the FBI was closely watching Local 248. Although the FBI officially avoided investigating labor unions, it was actually watching many hundreds of labor organizations, often coordinating its efforts with the HUAC. David Caute, *The Great Fear: The Anti-Communist Purge Under Truman and Eisenhower* (New York: Simon & Schuster, 1978), cites frequent incidents of this executive-legislative teamwork. The FBI and the Department of Justice were both intimately involved in the Local 248 Christoffel perjury case. One needs to emphasize that, according to standard federal procedure, in such litigation as the Christoffel case indictments and convictions do not take place without Justice approval and action, though suggestions may originate in the legislative body.

We have also seen that when President Reuther convened the new IEB immediately after the November 1947 convention, he made compliance with Taft-Hartley the most urgent item on the agenda. The board not only voted to comply with Taft-Hartley but instructed all locals to sign and file the affidavits. Local 248 did so.

Meeting again in December 1947, the new administration at UAW-CIO headquarters showed continuing insecurity about Local 248. The IEB was asked and voted to remove the incumbent Allis-Chalmers local officers, appointing in their stead the newly elected regional director, Pat Greathouse, to serve as an administrator over the local.[52] But even this post–Taft-Hartley action against Local 248 was not regarded as adequate for regaining control of the local. So at a subsequent special session called by the international president, where "the question before the Board [was] the situation in Local 248," the board voted unanimously (1) to concur with President Reuther's recommendation that the defense money previously voted for the defendants who had been cited by Congress and then prosecuted by the Department of Justice be cut from $2,500 per week to a maximum of $10,000 in all, and (2) to remove the 1937 charter under which Allis-Chalmers workers had been affiliated to the UAW-CIO. Whatever public claims Buse, Christoffel, Story, and Reuther made in 1947, the international union was now carrying out the objectives that government and industry had previously sought: eliminating the local leadership at the Allis-Chalmers local.

Having embarked on a program of affidavit signing, the new IEB majority found the political atmosphere in the United States conducive to both compliance and tighter discipline. All sides in the legislative and executive branches of government were now agreed that a local with communist officers should not be tolerated, even if a majority first voted to have a union and then proceeded to elect officers deemed to be communist. For an insecure union leadership, the new political climate and the new labor law proved to be important weapons. As Lee Romano testified, this state of affairs was manna from heaven for a new presiding officer in an international that retained and was troubled by a lively opposition.

[52]UAW-CIO International Executive Board, December 1947, minutes, pp. 593–4 (ALHUA). Summoned to appear before the IEB, Robert Buse stated that the three top incumbent officers of the local, himself included, had decided not to run for reelection, although each had submitted his affidavits immediately after the November convention. This, he said, signified their desire to comply with the Taft-Hartley Act. But he withdrew, he told the IEB, because their remaining in office would jeopardize the members: "The three officers were still 'under attack' from the federal government, the state Employment Relations Board, and the Allis-Chalmers Company" (ibid.).

For many years, the major employers had used divide-and-conquer strategies. Now the officialdom of most larger unions, who had sought to curb local unions from encouraging rank-and-file activity through, say, unofficial strikes under the Wagner Act (when such actions were generally protected), could curb both the internal opposition and unofficial strikes under Taft-Hartley.

Harris has described in his classic *The Right to Manage* the "Great Free Enterprise Campaign" whereby "the right to manage" was being implemented after Taft-Hartley. The Allis-Chalmers Company participated in that campaign through the "generously funded and broadly based" Foundation for Economic Education. The Allis-Chalmers Company was a major actor in the events leading up to Taft-Hartley's enactment; it continued its counteroffensive in the aftermath period by pursuing the prosecution of Christoffel and accommodating itself – for the moment – to the new international and local union leadership. The new political atmosphere helped.

By late 1947 the Truman administration was busy implementing its loyalty order. The states and many cities and some employers were decreeing their own loyalty programs. And many employers were finding that the new act was a convenient means of eliminating or taming the unions. The bulk of labor and the country at large were now embracing the emerging Truman Doctrine not only for international policy but to oust the "Reds" from unions, as Kennedy, Nixon, and others had urged.

The CIO and the UAW were in accord with the basic anticommunist premise of the Truman Doctrine. After the 1947 UAW convention, one sees the entire CIO shedding its former neutrality in the UAW factional alignment. The *CIO News*, under a new and avowedly right-wing editor, still showed considerable ambivalence in its reporting of domestic and foreign news. But the *News* implicitly advocated compliance with Section 9(h) by featuring editorials and news about the increasing number of affiliates (including many left-leaning affiliates) deciding to comply after the 1948 elections. It also featured stories and columns on NLRB-conducted elections that were designed to show that elections, even under Taft-Hartley, could favor the CIO. In addition, it increasingly displayed a pro-Truman, anti-CPUSA bias on domestic matters and a decidedly pronounced bias in reports on international affairs.[53]

Through all these internal and external developments, the international UAW-CIO tightened its controls and won approval from the Truman White House and the national CIO. But considerable anxiety was now surfacing not

---

[53]*CIO News.*

only within the customary left-center opposition in the UAW-CIO but among some noncommunist Reutherite colleagues. Frank Marquart, who had been educational director for several "pro-Reuther" locals, in a thoughtful book published in 1975 pinpointed the immediate period following enactment of Taft-Hartley as one during which the auto union had been "reduced to a one-party state with a hierarchy that controls the policy-making machinery." Of the much-vaunted "political action," he wrote that it "had become a property of the Democratic Party."[54] Allowing for Marquart's bias – he remained a Socialist Party member – this tendency was in accord with historic trends within unions whereby a mass organization eventually comes under a tight bureaucratic structure.

The so-called left-center caucus was disintegrating at local, regional, and international levels. Although the rank and file generally kept its power at the plants and remained disciplined, successive conventions repeatedly reelected the administration's slate of officers and board members. Apart from Reuther's capable leadership qualities, the incumbent international leadership was bolstered by rising output, high employment, and rising prices. Often these advances occurred without strikes or threats of strikes. But the union was now becoming a disciplinary arm of management.

I began this study with a brief analysis of the National Association of Manufacturers' historical view of labor relations and its vision of postwar, post–Wagner Act labor relations. We close with a brief look at the 1948 meeting of the manufacturers, where the politics of the 1946–7 strike at West Allis surfaced.

The bitter stoppage at Allis-Chalmers ended in defeat for the workers. Still, at the three-day National Association of Manufacturers' meeting on Taft-Hartley, that particular strike retained its importance for management. NLRB general counsel Robert H. Denham; Raymond Smethurst, the NAM lawyer who had been active behind the scenes in the legislative stages of Taft-Hartley; and Allis-Chalmers vice-president Harold Story were all present. Smethurst told this audience of organized, union-hostile employers about their victory in the 80th Congress and how they should make full use of the new law. Robert Denham, stepping out of his ostensibly neutral government role, denounced the International Typographical Union, which continued its refusal to sign the Section 9(h) affidavits, for a strike in which it was then

---

[54]Frank Marquart, *An Auto Worker's Journal* (University Park, Pa.: Pennsylvania State University Press, 1975), p. 125. Cf. Jack Stieber, *Governing the UAW* (New York: Wiley, 1962); Johnson, *Maurice Sugar*, pp. 257ff.

engaged. He praised employers for "valiantly" upholding the act. Association leader Frank Rising called for "management interference in the internal affairs of unions." He reportedly also told Vice-President Story that "his company had been the laughing stock" of labor-relations circles because it had waited so long to attack Local 248.[55]

This was unfair to Story and his company. We have seen how the NAM-affiliated Allis-Chalmers Company capitalized on the internal differences in the UAW-CIO when testifying in favor of Taft-Hartley. The company had also successfully resisted a new contract with the local. Finally, with international union cooperation, the firm had succeeded in eliminating the local from the West Allis plant altogether. Although neither its corporate future nor its relations with the local replacement were assured, it had a compliant union instead of a local that had managed to win significant power at the workplace.

Labor historians have generally avoided discussing the fragmentation effects of Taft-Hartley on those unions that remained in the CIO and then became part of the merged AFL-CIO; how Taft-Hartley's Section 9(h) was an important tool in 1947–50 for cleaning the left out of the CIO; and how the CIO affiliates' policies on affidavit signing and support for Truman in 1948 may have helped bring about ideological convergence with the AFL as well as White House approval.

The political atmosphere of the immediate postwar period did not prevent the United States from participating in the inclusive United Nations, but the anticommunist climate that helped produce a Republican majority in the 80th Congress brought about a new anticommunist world federation of unions sponsored by the AFL and the CIO, and led to support of both the president's loyalty program and Congress' affidavit requirement. That atmosphere, which helped bring about Taft-Hartley and Taft-Hartley compliance, also encouraged unions to implement heretofore unused constitutional barriers against communists.

The communist menace was no more than a *bobbe myseh* (Yiddish for "grandmother's tale"), but it acted as a potent influence throughout government, among the public, and within the labor movement. The real and not just rhetorical behavior of labor organizations demonstrates that the Labor-Management Relations (Taft-Hartley) Act diminished labor's power. Ironically, Taft-Hartley's Section 9(h) increased labor's compliance with a law that was designed to function against its own interest and helped pave the way for the McCarthy years.

---

[55]From the story in *The International Woodworker*, "NAM Plans to Crack Taft-Hartley Whip: CIO Termed 'Trial Balloon.'" This story was prepared and distributed by the Federated Press, a labor news service, and is credited by the *Woodworker*, a subscriber.

POSTLUDE

"Irv, we can't fight this. Walter says you hired the wife of the atomic spy. So for the good of the union, you should resign."

Unpublished remark by Richard T. Leonard, international vice-president, UAW-CIO, one day preceding the Louisville, Ky., meeting of the executive board, UAW-CIO, in March 1947

The official archives of the UAW-CIO in the Walter P. Reuther Library at Wayne State University do not contain these remarks by Richard Leonard. Nor were they officially reported in any other archival source, although the Reuther Library has extensive board minutes, along with a special mimeographed summary headed "Controversial Issues, International Executive Board, Louisville, Kentucky, March 5, 1947."

At a "Richter case" trial conducted by board members, the president of the UAW-CIO, Walter P. Reuther, chose not to include the spy charge in his list of official accusations. Therefore, one finds no mention of that part of his case in either of the two official records: the board minutes or the "Controversial Issues" report, both prepared by George F. Addes, the incumbent "anti-Reuther" secretary-treasurer of the UAW-CIO.

Most conscientious labor historians digging into the valuable Auto Workers collections at Wayne State understandably would rely on Addes' record. The incident is discussed here for three important reasons. First, both the official and the unreported records suggest my own leftist perspective on events of the period. Second, the case illustrates the general inadequacy of relying on official labor records to interpret labor history. Third, and perhaps most important, the entire incident, including the board meeting, provides insight into the disastrous effects on labor of the factionalism in the largest union in the United States at the time of the witch-hunt crisis.

The way in which my case was handled shows how little regard was paid to the needs of the labor movement as individual leaders in both UAW caucuses went about accommodating themselves to events and personal ambitions. The fate of qualified staffers, like the needs of many rank-and-file members, all too often became dispensable.

The press recognized Walter Reuther in 1945–7 as a labor leader of extraordinary ability and energy, as a man who by his ascent to the presidency of the UAW-CIO was a pivotal force in the entire CIO. The three metropolitan Detroit dailies had long seen in the youthful red-haired UAW leader a plausible alternative to the communist-supported incumbents. When Reuther defeated R. J. Thomas for the presidency in 1946, the national press jumped on the bandwagon. Alone among credible labor figures, "the Redhead" was willing and able to make communism the labor issue of the day.

Reuther was cautious in his approach to headline events, however. Although ready to brandish the atomic-spy charge against me privately – causing panic among some left-supported centrists to the point where they were ready to let me go – Reuther was astute enough not to make such a wild accusation in the public record. Conversely, the centrists on the board decided to confront their old protagonist only after their caucus leader, George F. Addes, and his group (including my immediate boss, Leonard) were convinced I could help them by appearing before the divided international executive board (IEB) to the spy charge and any other charges Reuther might level against me. I first convinced the Addes caucus of my innocence in an off-the-record meeting. Only then did that majority caucus agree to my being present at the UAW board meeting, over Reuther's objections.

Reuther's own real view of the Richter-case issue at Louisville was less ideological: As summed up in a story appearing in the *Detroit News* of March 24, 1947, under the byline of Asher Lauren, a reporter for a daily paper friendly to the new UAW president, Reuther believed that the union had to adapt to the Cold War climate, but his main concern was gaining control of the UAW. The headline over Lauren's story was "Reuther Asks Purge of Reds: Get House in Order, Union Board Told." This leaked story abstains altogether from mentioning the tenuous atomic-spy question. It focuses on Walter Reuther's serious conflict with the board majority over the staff, and the broader factional conflict over the new president's efforts to gain control of the still turbulent UAW-CIO. The board was still stopping him on both counts.

This story by a leading Detroit labor reporter illuminates what I now see as Reuther's main motivation all through this period: winning the conflict for control of the board, which meant wresting control from what he termed the mechanical majority.[1] He did just that at the November 1947 convention – a

---

[1] *Detroit News,* March 24, 1947, "Reuther Asks Purge of Reds," by Lauren Asher. International Executive Board, March 1947, minutes (ALHUA, box 7); cf. *Wage Earner,* weekly newspaper of the Association of Catholic Trade Unions, Detroit chapter, for 1946–7.

point that proved to be of crucial importance for the present analysis and, more immediately, for my UAW career.

Lauren and Reuther were careful to place their target in the context of a general witch hunt in Washington, the national CIO's conforming acts, and the consequent need for the UAW to conduct its own "purge of Reds" and "those inclining to the left."

There were already the beginnings of a witch hunt in Washington. This held threats for all labor, as President Walter Reuther told his board at Louisville. It will be recalled that the political climate had indeed changed. While Congress was taking advantage of that change to curb labor, it did so with clear aid from a divided labor movement. Like many other CIO leaders, Reuther was sufficiently attuned to politics to recognize that this change in the political climate could be devastating to the unions, especially those with left-wing officers and staff. He knew that the AFL-affiliated unions were outdistancing the rival CIO. The Federation had indicated its acceptance of the Taft-Hartley Act in spite of its fears. In doing so, it moved to the right, supported the antiradical drive as it had after World War I, and continued to view the CIO as Red even while courting some of its right-wing leaders.

The Richter case opened on the very same day that the Truman loyalty oath of 1947 was announced.[2] It predated the McCarthy hearings of the 1950s and subsequent widespread persecution of communist immigrants and other radicals. None of the UAW leaders had background and training comparable to Reuther's for combating such tendencies; but despite his socialist pro-Soviet past, he was not interested in or really worried about communism as a theory of government, as a political party, or as a distinctive influence in the Auto Workers, although he frequently discussed such issues. His immediate aim in 1947 was consolidating his control of the UAW-CIO. Eliminating the "Reds" was not an important step toward acquiring that control. As I said to Leonard, a former right-wing caucus member now temporarily in the Addes-Thomas

[2]The liberal Louisville *Courier Journal* of March 23, 1947, featured the March 22 Truman directive under a three-column headline on its front page reading "Truman Orders Purge of U.S. Employees with Dubious Loyalty"; directly under the banner headline, in a two-column headline, the same paper reported, "U.A.W. Factions Debate Firing Union's Lobbyist"; alongside my photo (with the caption "Tests U.A.W., peace") the story featured Reuther's allegation of "leftist influences" within the union, centering on Reuther's allegations and my defenders. Although most daily papers did not give it the front page, the "test" was reported by virtually all dailies; the *Ford Facts* editor as well as the three Detroit dailies carried inside stories, the former based on telephone interviews with me, the latter based on extended conversations with Reuther and his aides. Cf. *New York Times*, March 24, 1947, which headlined this event (too optimistically, as it turned out) on an inside page: "UAW Backs Richter to Stay as Lobbyist," with the subhead "Board Rejects Reuther View He Has 'Leftist Leanings' and Should Be Put Out."

caucus, "Walter isn't interested in me, he's after you and other UAW leaders standing in his way."

I first appeared at Louisville after I asked Leonard by phone to let me attend. He had called me in Washington the day before the meeting began to ask me to resign. "Walter has convinced me and all the boys that you should resign," Leonard said. I asked him for a delay until I could meet with him and the "boys" in Louisville, and he agreed.

Leonard's first words upon meeting me in the Louisville hotel where the board was convening were: "Irv, we can't fight this. Walter says you hired the wife of the atomic spy." The "atomic spy" was Carl Marzani. His name had been blazoned in countless headlines: Senator Patrick A. McCarran (D., Nev.) had attached a rider to the State Department's appropriations in 1946 calling for Marzani's dismissal. McCarran's move had been accompanied by newspaper stories from Capitol Hill alleging that through his Communist Party associations Marzani had helped the Soviet Union learn about U.S. atomic secrets.[3]

Perhaps the UAW-CIO president and other officials became unduly frightened by the politics of the Marzani case; if so, they were not alone. According to an unpublished dissertation by Peter H. Irons, Marzani's troubles began when he produced a film, *Deadline for Action,* for the CIO-affiliated United Electric, Radio and Machine Workers (UE) during that union's early-1946 strike against General Electric. Marzani's film touched a highly sensitive chord by focusing attention on GE's alleged wartime ties with Nazi Germany's industrialists. On December 20, 1946, Marzani was discharged from the State Department, where he had gone after wartime service in the Office of Strategic Services. In 1947 he was convicted of perjury after he denied being a member of the Communist Party while employed by the U.S. government.

As Irons noted in his dissertation, Marzani's discharge and conviction occurred two years before the more famous Hiss case; Irons wrote that it surfaced "as a way of persuading the public that subversion in government was an imminent problem and of adding pressure on Truman for a full-scale loyalty program."[4] This executive-branch program was of course inimical to leftism in general, but it also influenced private-sector employees, employers, and unions.

[3]David Caute, *The Great Fear: The Anti-Communist Purge Under Truman and Eisenhower* (New York: Simon & Schuster, 1978), pp. 304, 376.
[4]Peter Hanlon Irons, "America's Cold War Crusade: Domestic Politics and Foreign Policy, 1942–1958" (doctoral dissertation, Boston University, 1972). Cf. I. F. Stone, "A New Weapon for Witch Hunters," *Nation,* July 12, 1947.

The informal allegation made to Leonard by Reuther was that Marzani's wife, Edith, whom I had hired to do secretarial work, was evidence of my involvement with the "atomic spy." This was enough for both factions – the left, of which Leonard was then a part, as well as the right – to insist that I must go. When Leonard confronted me with this charge, I admitted that I had hired Edith Marzani; that in fact she was a temporary replacement for a regular secretary who was on vacation; and that – this was the clincher for Leonard – she had first appeared in the Washington office as a replacement for one of the secretaries in the "Reuther" Consumer Department headed by Donald Montgomery. A well-known economist, Montgomery had become Reuther's top brains-truster in the UAW-CIO Washington office and his chief liaison with the national CIO offices. Leonard responded to my explanation with a sigh of relief: "Well, that answers the tough one. But Walter also says that you were disloyal to the CIO by supporting the May-Bailey bill, which the Communist Party supported."

The May-Bailey bill incorporated President Roosevelt's idea for a national manpower draft during the war. It was supported by an important block of left-wing board members of the CIO, notably Harry Bridges, president of the International Warehousemen's and Longshoremen's Union. Bridges' rationale was that FDR's plans for winning the war, including his ideas on assuring manpower, should be given full backing. However, after CIO president Philip Murray spoke out strongly against the measure, the CIO board voted down Bridges' motion of support. Thus, official CIO policy was clearly in opposition to May-Bailey. My reply to Leonard on this point was that I had not only opposed the bill but had helped devise CIO strategies to defeat it; that I could provide evidence to the boys – the majority of the UAW-CIO board. Finally, Leonard said, "Walter has convinced a lot of us that Congress won't work with you any more." Again I replied that this was unwarranted; that I had with me documentary evidence to prove the contrary, and in fact some members of Congress were willing to come to Louisville to vouch for me. At that point, Leonard, with a great sigh of satisfaction, suggested I should talk to the boys.

I then addressed the so-called left caucus in a special meeting convened by George Addes. After hearing my rebuttal to Reuther's accusations and getting from Addes a nod of his head, that mechanical-majority caucus voted unanimously – but with no official transcript or recorded vote – to have me attend the board meeting to hear and answer whatever charges Reuther would present. (George Addes chaired the caucus meeting; R. J. Thomas was present but not in a caucus leadership role.)

At the official board meeting in Louisville, the president of the union, acting as prosecutor, made no mention of the Marzani matter.[5] Instead, he focused on the issue of the May-Bailey bill in an attempt to demonstrate that I had been "disloyal" to the CIO and the UAW-CIO in supporting that legislation. But I had known from stories appearing for weeks prior to the board meeting in the weekly newspaper of the right-wing caucus, the *Wage Earner* (published in Detroit by the Association of Catholic Trade Unionists), that the May-Bailey story was being leaked by headquarters to, and was circulating in, key locals. So I was prepared to answer, and I responded by reading from congressional and union documentary evidence that verified my loyalty on this matter and other CIO positions.

After hearing all the official charges made by Reuther and my rebuttal of them, board member Percy Llewelyn of the majority caucus, with support from Leonard, officially moved that my "report" be approved and "that the Board express itself in the ability, loyalty, and effectiveness of the legislative ability of Richter."[6] Expressing outrage about what such a motion might do to the image of the new president, board member Richard Gosser asked for "some other better worded recommendation."[7] The Llewelyn initiative failed. Subsequently there was an official motion to set up an "investigating committee" to look into the charges against me. That also was defeated. Then followed agreement by all on a motion made by Leonard that was conditional on a unanimous vote of the board: "The allegations presented to the International Executive Board regarding disloyal activities on the part of Irving Richter have not been substantiated, therefore, the International Executive Board finds no cause for action."[8]

Thus, without confronting the issue of central executive authority in the union or the more important question of how the UAW-CIO should behave in response to the threat of the Washington witch hunts, the entire board simply decided there was no basis for the highly publicized charges against Richter, the sole Washington legislative representative of the largest union in the country. The board members, including the so-called left, were content to drop the matter. For the opposition group, scoring a paper victory over "the Redhead" was apparently enough.

My own head, although exposed, was not yet chopped off. That happened later in the year, after Reuther won a majority on the board at the 1947

[5]UAW-CIO International Executive Board, Louisville, March 22, 1947, minutes, p. 167 (AL-HUA). Reuther's charges are on pp. 37–41, under the heading "Status of Irving Richter." Reuther's discussion, my defense, and discussions by various board members – all edited by Secretary-Treasurer George F. Addes and his staff – occupy pages 156–84 of those minutes.
[6]Ibid., p. 185. [7]Ibid., p. 186. [8]Ibid.

international convention. Despite my having been unanimously cleared of charges in March, I was discharged in November by a letter from the president, without a hearing or debate, without notice or severance pay.

In view of the election of a right-winger to the presidency in 1946, vast changes in the national political climate together with a hastening of the national CIO move to the right, and Reuther's sweeping officers and other opposition members off the executive board at the UAW 1947 convention, my being discharged was probably inevitable. But, ironically, I undoubtedly contributed to my dismissal by my active role in the spring of 1947 against what Reuther and others called the slave-labor bill, the Taft-Hartley substitute for the National Labor Relations Act. The Wagner Act, labor's Magna Carta, which of all New Deal laws was most cherished by the CIO and the UAW, had been influential in the creation of the auto workers' union and other CIO unions. But, as noted in my two chapters on Taft-Hartley, not all CIO factions, and only a few in the AFL, actually fought against passage of this bill or worked for repeal. The international president of the UAW-CIO capitalized on the "loyalty" or "noncommunist" Section 9(h) to consolidate his power over the turbulent, faction-ridden Auto Workers.

My "trial" took place shortly after the Taft-Hartley Act was passed and President Truman's veto was overridden. Paradoxically, though I took a leading role against that measure, I was apparently too keen on criticizing pro–Taft-Hartley voices in the leadership. I acted in a way that added further to my troubles. At several local union meetings I addressed in the summer and fall of 1947, I challenged the wisdom of the decision by Reuther and Emil Mazey to accommodate themselves to the Taft-Hartley Act by signing noncommunist affidavits.[9] (Nonaccommodation was still the official CIO position at the time.) Reuther and Mazey argued that the affidavits should be signed by the UAW – even while they knew that those accused of being communist could not sign without great personal risk – so that the union could continue to use the services of the reconstructed National Labor Relations Board.

What is the point of recounting the UAW's "Richter case"? After all, the trial ordered by the IEB saved my job only briefly. The case occurred forty

[9]Ironically, during the trial I read into the record a 1947 "Dear Irv" letter from Emil Mazey, then director of veterans' affairs for the UAW, thanking me for "making appointments" and for my "talk on the procedure to be followed by the delegates in contacting their Congressmen which was greatly appreciated by delegates attending this conference" (letter dated February 6, 1947, IEB, March 22, 1947, minutes, p. 166. Mazey was referring to a UAW-CIO veterans' conference he had arranged in Washington.

years ago. Most of the principals are dead.[10] In the meantime, the UAW-CIO, like most unions involved in mass-production industries, has undergone many changes in membership and leadership, made gains in bargaining and other policies, and even changed its affiliations at home and abroad. The CIO itself has been merged with the older American Federation of Labor into today's American Federation of Labor–Congress of Industrial Organizations, affiliated with the International Confederation of Free Trade Unions.[11]

Yet in the end, I think the effort of writing – and reading – this may be justified. It does indicate how incomplete, if not inaccurate, official labor records can be; it does show my own leftist leanings. It also provides an unusually close look at a major union's succumbing to its own factionalism and forsaking any serious resistance to the witch-hunt, or loyalty, investigations in Washington.

---

[10]For a scholarly but incomplete treatment of the Richter case, see Roger R. Keeran, *The Communist Party and the Auto Workers Unions* (Bloomington: Indiana University Press, 1980), pp. 80–2.

[11]AFL-CIO Committee on the Evolution of Work, "The Changing Situation of Workers and Their Unions" (report, 1985), p. 1 (AFL-CIO Library); cf. Richard B. Freeman and James L. Medoff, "New Estimates of Private Sector Unionism in the United States," *Industrial and Labor Relations Review,* 32, no. 2 (January 1979); Irving Richter, "American Labor" (article based on discussion led by Richter and including participation by labor leaders at the Center for the Study of Democratic Institutions), *Center Magazine,* May–June 1979, pp. 34ff.

INDEX

"ACTION" booklet (Bradford), 27
ACTU, *see* Association of Catholic Trade
  Unionists
Addes, George F., viii, xx–xxi, 11, 114,
  122, 125n45, 128, 134, 135; anticommu-
  nism, 74; and left-center coalition, 12, 74,
  93; and mechanical majority, 65; and
  Richter case, 138; and UAW factionalism,
  21, 122, 123, 124, 126
Addes-Thomas (center-left) coalition, 74, 93
Adelman, Meyer, 83
AFL, *see* American Federation of Labor
African-Americans, 79; *see also* blacks
Aiken, George D., 59, 60
Allis-Chalmers Company, 54, 55, 56, 62–3,
  64–5, 67, 132–3; corporate testimony, 72,
  73–84; and enactment of Taft-Hartley,
  131; opposition to unions, 93; politiciza-
  tion of strike against, 71; *see also* United
  Auto Workers Local 248 (Allis-Chalmers)
  strike
Amalgamated Clothing Workers (ACW), 13,
  24
Amalgamated Meatcutters and Butcher
  Workmen of North America (AFL), 115
American Democracy, The (Laski), 13
American Federation of Labor (AFL), xi,
  xii, xiv, 15, 16, 63; and affidavit requirement, 94; affiliated unions, 3, 4, 5; and
  CIO, 6, 56, 101, 107–8, 133, 141; divisions in, xxi; executive council, 104, 106;
  "federal" locals, 71; and government intervention, 58, 59; ideological conformity in
  international affairs, 34; Lewis and, 42; as
  model of labor organization, xvii, xviii;
  and NLRB, 7; and no-strike pledge, 8, 20;
  and political action, xx, 2–3, 9, 10–11;
  power of, 13–14; response to Taft-Hartley,
  xiv–xv, 48, 101–7; strikes, 19, 55, 61;
  support for Truman, 96; withdrawal from
  Management-Labor Charter, 29–34

American flag, 63
Americanism (issue), 54, 55, 56
American Plan, 4
anticommunism, xv, 12, 77, 89; in AFL, 34;
  in Allis-Chalmers corporate testimony, 73–
  4; and anti-Semitism, 118; of Catholic
  Church, 110–11; postwar, 133; strikes
  and, 70
anti-injunction law, 69
anti-Semitism, 118
Association of Catholic Trade Unionists
  (ACTU), 10–11, 32, 62, 63, 122, 128, 129
Atwood, Arnold, 126
auto industry: strikes in, 51
Automobile, Aircraft, and Agricultural
  Workers of America, 64; *and see* United
  Auto Workers

Baldenzi, George, 24
Barkley, Alben W., 59
Belkin, Louis S., 107
Bevin, Ernest, 13
"Big Labor" (concept), 1, 8, 13
Big Three in CIO, 58
bill of rights for workers, 69, 94, 103
Bittner, Van, 83
blacks, 9, 79, 114, 116–117, 118
Bowles, Chester, x, 17
boycott(s), 119; secondary, vii
Bradford, Ralph, 27–8
Bridges, Harry, 75, 138
Briggs Manufacturing, 51
Brotherhood of Railroad Trainmen (BRT),
  35–6; *see also* railroad brotherhoods
Browder, Earl, 88
BRT, *see* Brotherhood of Railroad Trainmen
building trades unions, 69, 105
Bureau of Labor Statistics (BLS), 48–9, 50,
  61, 112
Buse, Robert, 60, 66, 81, 83–4, 85, 88, 89,
  91; scapegoated, 129, 130

143